GOD IS
ROUND

JUAN VILLORO

GOD IS ROUND

TACKLING THE GIANTS, VILLAINS,
TRIUMPHS, AND SCANDALS OF
THE WORLD'S FAVORITE GAME

Translated from the Spanish by
Thomas Bunstead

RESTLESS BOOKS
BROOKLYN, NEW YORK

In the beginning, God went to school and used to go and play football with his friends until classes started. Though God knows a lot, He always wants to learn and try new things. One day God said: "I've worked hard today, it's time to go and play." God and his friend started playing football and at one point God kicked the ball so hard that it flew into a rosebush and burst. The explosion created the universe and everything around us.

—RODRIGO NAVARRO MORALES, AGE SEVEN

This noise truly is an irritation, this match that seeps into my life once more when my only aim is to pay my dues and grow old with dignity. That is the aim of an Olympian, Goethian intellectual. And as I proceed to write, the beast of the terraces re-emerges, the militant Barcelona supporter, the fan of the club that, before it became a property developer, was more than a club.

—MANUEL VÁZQUEZ MONTALBÁN

Pythagoras used to say that life resembles the Olympic Games: a few people strain their muscles to carry off a prize; others bring trinkets to sell to the crowd for gain; and some there are, and not the worst, who seek no other profit than to look at the show and see how and why everything is done; spectators of the life of other people in order to judge and regulate their own.

—MONTAIGNE

And who told you that the gods may not cooperate with us?

—MARCUS AURELIUS

PAPERBACK ISBN: 978-1-63206-0-587
ELECTRONIC: 978-1-63206-0-778

Printed in the United States of America

Ellison, Stavans, and Hochstein LP
232 3rd Street, Suite A111
Brooklyn, NY 11215
www.restlessbooks.com
publisher@restlessbooks.com

CONTENTS

ONETTI THE TICKET VENDOR

IN THE DAYS when literary types were heavy smokers, Juan Carlos Onetti reinvented the art of breathing. The Uruguayan writer had a smooth and firm lilt, which was necessary given the painful subject he always tackled: the truth. His conspiratorial, compassionate tone was a great softener. His characters embark on dead-end projects and senseless love affairs, struggling to impose a logic that only seems apparent to them. In the world of facts they always lose, but they maintain their dignity in pitting themselves against all evidence.

Curiously enough, this maker of supremely devastating fictions was at one time a seller of dreams. A letter dated July 10, 1937 included the following: "No news—except for a job offer: I'm going to be selling tickets at the national football stadium. It looks like I start on Sunday."

Hugo Verani brought the correspondence to light in 2009. The author of *A Brief Life* was writing to the Argentine painter and art critic Julio E. Payró, to whom he dedicated *No Man's Land* no less than twice (first inscribing his friend's name and twenty-four years later adding "with all my hate").

Onetti worked as a brick carrier, a painter-decorator, a porter, and a door-to-door salesman of calculators and drills before moving on to the demands of journalism (he was known to have slept at the newspaper offices at times). The strangest job he ever had was the one at the Estadio Centenario. In a magnificent irony, the job had been given to an inventor of defeats.

In *Letters to a Young Writer*, the novelist recommends the view of Montevideo "from the stadium flagpole": "Before me, the town; above me the proud, fluttering flag bearing the historic insignia, recalling the glorious afternoons of 4–0, 4–2, and 3–1, the glory among the howls, the hats, the bottles, and the oranges." (He alludes to results that include Uruguay's 4–2 victory over Argentina in the 1930 World Cup Final.)

In the letters he writes of his "absolute lack of faith." His furious skepticism drove him at one point to write, "a cynical indifference is coming to fruition inside me." Football has been served by writers in a great many different ways (not excluding by some writers' total ignorance of the game). In Onetti's case, the job at the stadium provided him with an ironic emotional counterweight: "I go to the stadium to form my own mass sensibility, multitudinous and at the same time unanimous." Nothing could have been more foreign to the author of *The Shipyard* than unanimity, but the pull of this enthusiastic temptation can be seen when we read him say he's going *"raja pal jurgo"*—a very slangy, working-class way of saying "off to the match."

The letters also reveal that he wrote a play in 1937 that was later lost: *Napoleon's Island*. True to form, Onetti chose to write about the emperor after his downfall, when all he commanded was censure and rebukes.

What kind of football fan was Onetti? In another letter he says, "A character in my boring book makes an *apologia* for a fantasy island to a downbeat woman. She listens, and then says: 'But that's all lies, isn't it?' Downcast, he admits that she's right. The woman smiles. 'But it doesn't matter,' she says. 'The island's a lovely place all the same. Don't you think?'" There are such things as necessary lies, soothing deceitfulness—surely this was how Onetti saw football matches. César Luis Menotti was in agreement: "A football stadium," he said, "is the only place where I like to be deceived."

In his books, and in the Centenario, Onetti enters environments that are enhanced by what we believe about them, and he also showed that glory is, in the end, a modest cause, something that takes place "among the howls, the hats, the bottles, and the oranges."

It would be an absurd sort of vanity to call oneself a disciple of Onetti; after all, there's only one master. All my reading has, however, led me to form a more minor delusion: I see him not as the manager who picked me to play, nor even as the star striker to whom I only need pass the ball. His legacy came to me in a simpler way, in keeping with the job he held for a short time: a ticket vendor.

I picture a sunny afternoon, him handing me my stub by the turnstiles, like a letter of safe passage that allows me to pass over the books and dive right into the stadium. And he does it with the most wonderful indifference, refusing to take responsibility for the consequences. Onetti's books convinced me that the writing dream is a possibility.

This book combines a passion for literature and a passion for football. It would not exist if it weren't for the on-pitch wizards, but just as crucial were the masters who convinced me of a certain axiom: reality gets better in the writing of it.

"Among the howls, the hats, the bottles, and the oranges," the match gets underway.

WINTER CHAMPION:
FANDOM IN THE FIRST PERSON

IF THERE WERE TO BE A World Cup between football supporters, Mexico vs. Scotland would be a possible final. Neither country has ever done well on an international stage and, perhaps because of that, each has opted for the compensatory pleasure of filling stadiums instead.

Since I was a child I've been aware that the matches I watch aren't the best. The sensation of being far from truly great endeavors intensified when satellite TV began bringing goals to us from distant lands. But in any case, being a Mexico supporter, I've always known that one's passion for the game has little to do with winning all the time.

When deciding which team to support you also decide the nature of your Sundays to come. Some will opt for a solid, familiar, popular side, while others, naturally enough, choose the most successful team at the time. Sometimes destiny takes the form of a regional fatalism, and before the person in question becomes conscious of their free will, the fan is born, Athens-like, determined by city.

Other times the choice is more random, like when the fan experiences love (of a player) at first sight—some bewitching idol who condenses all the hopes and dreams of youth. Nothing hurts like when a favorite player leaves for another club, having been such a focal point for the dreams of the supporters. But when it does happen, the fan will almost always stay faithful to the club, no matter how much of the initial motivation has left. The fan scans among the eleven ghosts now playing for the club, his or her attitude one of resignation as he or she tries to discern the magic of that first genius. At this point the game becomes "merely" a team game, no "I" in it until the apostate comes back to represent his new club, showing his face at the pitch where he was once a ninety-minute god. Then the people who used to worship at his feet taste something bitter in their mouths, the bitter saliva of discord, as they understand, with a great and lucid bitterness, that the one out there doing the heroics is not one of them, and perhaps never was.

It's an unhappy afternoon, and one in which the young fan becomes a man, passing through the rite that sunders any desire for perfection, coming to understand that there's no such thing as an unconditional hero, and that the quality of his interest has changed: a team, an abstraction of colors, taking the place of that search for individual qualities.

Sometimes football attachments can begin with support of a certain shirt, regardless of who wears it. It's the look and not the spirit of a side that captivates skin-deep fans, fanatics for certain stripes over others. Such textile-based attraction is in some ways more likely to last. Besmirched the shirt might be by advertising, but the enthusiast of the chromatic school will always have this perennial belief to fall back on.

Once the pulse has been set, the team decided, there's no going back. Though there are examples of those for whom rationality has intervened, the purebred fanatic does not renounce his own, even if the team gets trounced. It may be that football represents the final legitimate frontier of emotional intransigence; overcoming it would mean betraying one's infancy, refusing the child who understood that heroes either dress in white, or they dress in *blaugrana*.

In this changeable reality of ours, it's perfectly acceptable to switch ideology, job, or even, after one form of therapy or another, one's sex or religion. But to betray the activity that Javier Marías has defined as "the weekly return to childhood," now that's a thorny thing. Which person, having placed all their hopes in a team, can entertain a change of heart during adulthood, the very abolition of which is what football stands for?

COMPLICATED PASSIONS: BARCA AND NECAXA

Like so many others, I was born under the passional obligation to support a club that was "more than a club." My father was born in Barcelona, and when he left, at the age of ten, he was convinced of the fundamental importance of lateral passes, it being the cross-city avenue known as La Diagonal that led to Camp Nou. The first present I was ever given was a Barca key ring. It wasn't until I was six, in 1962, that I got to see "my" team play, on their tour of Mexico. There's something touching about supporting an invisible team. Still, every now and then, passion requires proof.

In addition to Barcelona, I had a liking for a team that was to give a different hue to my Sundays. My father, first and foremost a man of the academy, supported the University side, Los Pumas, but in my choice of a local team I didn't follow him. I studied at the German College, where reality became strange in all those long sequences of subordinate clauses. For some unfathomable reason I fell in with the Germans. We spoke only Spanish in the schoolyard. Kicking a ball and shouting in my own language went hand in hand. During those nine years, every second of which I counted, I looked out the classroom window at the yard, where jumpers stood in for goalposts. That rectangle was freedom, and it was my language. If I learned anything from the German College's arduous pedagogy, it was that I love nothing as much as Spanish. Just as attachments come into being by complete chance, I forever associated the pleasure I took in shouting in the outlawed language with the game that gave our playtimes meaning.

So football presented itself as my first urge to belong. Everyone in my neighborhood supported Necaxa, the electricians' team. They weren't exactly the logical option; not being much of a side, they were hardly guaranteed titles, nor were the Sundays going to be plain sailing. No one in the barrio had family in the syndicate of electricians, nor had anyone even been out to Necaxa, a town that had been flooded to make a dam to feed a power plant. Our floodlights might have hailed from Necaxa, but we weren't sophisticated enough to realize it (like when I first read *Moby Dick* and didn't know that whales were hunted to make candles from their sperm: it wasn't the quest for light that captivated me but Captain Ahab's fanatical gaze and his foam-flecked beard).

Why on earth did my neighbors support Necaxa? I never knew. To this day I've never visited the town, and simply take on trust the legend that when the water level drops in the dam during droughts, it reveals the bell tower of a church.

In fifty-seven years Necaxa never won the league and were relegated from the first division on two occasions (the second during my teens, when my team was substituted for by Atlético Español and came back up two years later with a different nickname, Los Rayos—the Rays). Nowadays this most gypsy of clubs plays in Aguascalientes, which to fans within Mexico City constitutes a kind of Patagonia. And yet this is the side that one night beat Pelé's Santos side; where "Fu Manchu" Reynoso was given his nickname upon making a ball vanish from the pitch; where Álex Aguinaga, a weary gladiator who gasped as he ran, dragged his team to a title that surpassed belief. We Necaxistas never needed to see a church submerged in a dam to believe in it. On the miracle days, the bells toll there.

Some people identify with the vastness of a continent and support América (or the money and TV fame this name represents in Mexico). I was looking for an attachment that was not quite so broad. My parents came from separatist traditions (her the Yucatán, him Catalonia), and it's no great surprise they divorced early. By way of contrast, I decided to be of my street.

Necaxa, ever movable, has been an auspicious team in the eyes of immigrants. In the 1960s it was the Jewish community's favorite side, as they didn't have their own pitch and had to train at the Club Deportivo Israelita. Nowadays Necaxa has a big Japanese following in Aguascalientes, with its new Nissan plant. Life is so strange that it even has curious ways of turning logical: after all, what could be more normal, in a sense, than the Rays awakening sympathies in people who hail from the land of the rising sun?

When Necaxa won a cup final in my childhood, beating América, the team everyone loved to hate, I felt the startling sensation of being on the wrong side in the battle. The electricians weren't proponents of masochism, but nor were they vain triumphalists. What they were good at was playing good football and doing surprising things on the pitch. For such artists of the unexpected, the scoreboard was of little concern. This peculiarity became all the more serious in the 1990s, when Los Rayos transformed into a powerful club. All that efficiency seemed like a vulgar transgression.

The psychology of fans is defined by the eleven players they support. Mercurial Necaxa is my street's team. It matters little that this slice of the city might have changed, or that I don't live there anymore. In Mexico City the sense of belonging doesn't depend on the people or the scenery. Everyone leaves, everything subsides. For us a street is what was (childhood, Necaxa). And that's why it matters.

WRITING FOOTBALL

It's unlikely you'll be a fan of any sport that you haven't felt the urge to play. I played quite a bit, including on Pumas youth teams. At the age of sixteen, I knew I wasn't going to make it as a top player, and that if I were ever to score at the Maracanã it would only be in my dreams.

Writing about football is one of the many consolations of literature. Every so often a critic will wonder how it is that no great football novel has ever been written on a planet that holds its breath during a World Cup. The answer seems fairly simple to me: the system of references in football is so strictly codified, and involves the emotions so totally, that it includes its own epic, its own tragedy, and its own comedy. There isn't any need for parallel dramas, and the writer's invention is left with very little space to work in. This is one of the reasons why we get better short stories about football than novels. Because football comes to us with all these preformed narratives, any hidden aspects, anything that hasn't already been published, tend to be minimal. The novelist, who sees the task as doing more than acting as a mirror, would rather look elsewhere for material. Whereas the short-story writer—interested in going back and recounting what has already happened—finds an inexhaustible fount.

And the fact is, football, in and of itself, is a question of words. Few activities depend so wholly on what is already known as this art of reiterating great feats on the field of play. The legends recounted by fans prolong the acts in a kind of nonstop passion that then stands in for the game, this munificent, purely weekend God.

In the games of my childhood, the fundamental aspect was the TV commentator, the great Ángel Fernández, who had it within him to turn a quite inglorious game into the fall of Carthage.

Commentators must be endowed with great imaginative capacities—as proved by the fact that some legendary rhapsodists even imparted games they never saw. Cristino Lorenzo was all but blind when he wove his magical accounts from Café Tupinamba in Mexico City; Pedro "The Wizard" Septién and other spellbinding radio commentators had to rely on telegrams to impart the details of baseball, boxing, and football.

Sadly, Homer doesn't always get a World Cup press pass, and commentaries are often very bland. Not that there's ever any lack of town criers, theorizers, or preachers in this sport. Football demands words, and not only well-crafted words; any fan equipped with that smug, dramatic apparatus, the mouth, gets to have his or her say. Why do we never shut up? Because football is so full of the downright incomprehensible. Out of the blue, a brilliant, battle-hardened player squanders a chance that even the commentator could have put away; a goalkeeper with nerves of steel will come out with gloves made of butter; a vastly experienced team will lose its mojo, or its attitude, or whatever we want to call the mysterious energy that unites them.

It's up to journalists to offer answers that convert these strange occurrences into something believable—though often the reasons they supply are frankly esoteric: the wrong ointment was applied to an abductor, the team's change kit was so garish it made them miss those penalties, the goalkeeper's teddy bear mascot was kicked by a photographer (from another newspaper).

WHEN WISHING HELPS

Stadiums, these theaters of dreams, fill up not only for what happens on the pitch. The people in the crowd charge a match with their own superstitions, desires, vengeful wishes, the most tremendous complexes, and legends of enormous intricacy. Football takes place both on the turf and inside the agitated awareness of the spectators. A sports report is a way of joining these two territories together.

The beautiful game can either fall within the sphere of inoffensive pleasures or flow out into the fanaticism of the hooligan, the arrogance of high-powered executives, or television's prefabricated lies. A mirror for the world beyond the stadiums, football is no stranger to violence, racism, or commercialization. The aporia of fans is pure and uncontaminated passion, one that repels the effects of beer, the mockery of the enemy, and the manipulation of the press. It is this rare thing that remains football's essential, redemptive motor. Far away from the multimillion-dollar signings, off on some nameless beach, someone is kicking a ball around, or something that stands in for a ball (a bundle of cloth, a can, a plastic bag full of paper). This expression transmits an inexpressible pleasure: that of playing for the sake of playing.

Walter Benjamin recalled that children do not define adults in terms of their powerfulness, but in terms of their "incapacity for magic"—they have lost contact with the primary kingdom of possible wonders. The phrase of the Brothers Grimm is worth remembering here: "In olden times, when wishing was still helpful..." Children's tales are instruments of return, ways back to the epoch in which wishes might still have an effect on reality.

In a state of perpetual infancy, the football fan casts around for magic powers. Gazing down on a spectacle heavy with performance-enhancing drugs, mass marketing, and the boorish and despicable deeds of the Ultras, the fan can still find there the unknown beach and a player juggling the ball for the fun of it.

As Giorgio Agamben has it, the wizard's grace derives from the fact one needn't earn the right to contemplate it: the gifts that ensue arrive arbitrarily, by chance. The great intercessors—Pelé, Didi, Maradona, Di Stéfano, Zidane, Ronaldo, Ronaldinho—didn't score their goals to reward the good conduct of their followers. With them, the magic came about *just because*—as the gift at the end of the fairy tale.

The inclination to kick things in order to diffuse emotions gives rise to all kinds of misgivings. It isn't only personal biographies that are retraced, but those of the species—toward an earlier step when hands were not yet predominant. Is this return impulse so important? Well, can we do without childhood, or the tribes we hail from? Modern culture privileges childhood, but considers the primal hordes to be suspect. Football puts us in touch with the innocence of hero seekers, but it also sets fire to things in the stands. The savages of postindustrial society paint their faces, tattoo their bodies, and chant strange slogans. This rowdy tribal aspect seems just as important to me as the preservation of childish ways of seeing. One of football's great mysteries is that it ritualizes passion and tribal attachments in addition to providing a container for them. There are so many occasions when it might spill over, but only on the worst does it do so.

In his staggering report on hooliganism, *Among the Thugs*, Bill Buford commits a decisive error of judgment. He attributes a legendary brawl between two sets of fans to the preceding match ending 0–0. In Buford's view, the tribe always needs a victor: the held tension had to come out in another way, and so unleashed this violence.

But there is no such thing as a pure witness, and Buford's judgment reveals where he's from: the US, a place where sports never end 0–0. In an environment utterly conditioned by competitiveness (the fans there raise their index fingers to signal the thing they want to be: number one), having a certified winner (even if it happens to be the other side) is always preferable to coming out even. Uncertainty and triumphalism don't mix.

And yet all football fans have memories of great matches that have ended in draws. In his Italia '90 book *All Played Out*, Pete Davies dedicates a chapter to the 1–1 between England and Germany, which had to be decided on penalties. The chapter is entitled "The Beautiful Game," in reference to what went on *before* the shootout (Germany went through). For a football fan, there's absolutely zero dishonor in sharing the spoils.

You get ardent fans, melancholic fans, fans with heart problems, and nostalgic fans, but above all, and surprisingly enough, a fan is *a person who resigns himself to things*. A stadium, that cauldron of voices and flares, might not seem like an incubator for stoicism, and yet it very much promotes coolness in the face of adversity. The referee gets a lot of things wrong, the turf becomes slippery, the most accurate player on your team misses every now and then. A whole catalog of imponderables, all kinds of surprises, can happen in football to put a dent in our mood; no one goes expecting the sure thing. As much as he or she complains about the opposing side, and sometimes about the not-opposing side, too, the spectator tacitly accepts that the unimaginable is what they've come to witness, and it won't be pretty. The equivalent would be going to a concert where brawls break out amongst the orchestra, the violinists are off key, and only from time to time does the rare miracle of a bit of music occur. This is the way with football: it doesn't happen, or half-happens, or happens just in the way you don't want it to happen, but constantly teeters on the edge of coming together *just right*.

Certain crowds play their role of attentive extras better than others. I once went to the Buenos Aires *clásico*, Boca Juniors vs. River Plate. A man, noting my Mexican accent, wanted to check something he'd been told by some Argentine friends: "Is it really true that in Mexico a fan of a team like Boca can watch the match standing next to fans of a team like River?" I said yes, it was. "And they don't end up murdering one another?" I admitted that, at least when it came to matters of football, we were fairly peace loving. "What degenerates!" came his unforgettable response.

Usually, a football stadium is made up of thousands of people so utterly disappointed with what they have just seen that all they're left to do is ruminate upon despair.

One of football's happiest legends is the idea of the crowd representing the "twelfth man." In his biography of Boca Juniors, Martín Caparrós says that the concept first occurred in the 1920s to the reporter Pablo Rojas Paz. His boss, Natalio Botana, the director of *Crítica*, asked him to prettify a match. In those days, if someone didn't attend a match, they only knew about the goals through hearsay, or from written accounts. "Football was, first and foremost, a story," writes Caparrós. And a story that was unconvincing, one that wouldn't be believed, would be forgotten. As well as a way with words, Rojas Paz had a boss with the sonorous name of a dictator of some tropical island. How could he disobey Natalio Botana, who foresaw the potential for roaring business on the football pages? Like so many desperate copywriters, Rojas Paz got excited in order to get others excited. He spoke of the "twelfth man" in times when the pitches were flat expanses with no witnesses other than the players' families or their creditors. But the metaphor was destined to become a reality, a way of explaining what in the future would come to be known as "playing at home."

There's no doubt that fans have a hand in deciding scores. But they still aren't the ones shooting on goal. Which means the substance of their inputs consists of swings between total dedication and abject acquiescence. Fans of Real Betis have an

Andalusian-inflected chant—"*manque pierda*"—which expresses their thick-and-thin support for the team, even in the unusual instance of a win. The Guadalajara side, Atlas, have the same chant, in Mexican Spanish: it's not unusual to hear "*aunque pierda*" echoing around their stands.

Something about one of football's partial attainments, that of being top of the league at Christmas, or "winter champion," has always spoken to me. A conquest with no purpose, or one that no longer serves a purpose.

Many different leagues have a break at Christmas. The first set of matches ends there. This idea has been lost in Mexico and other countries where greed has led to constant off-season minitournaments and the anointing of two champions a year.

In the long seasons that are football's true province, the winter champion is the leader who's yet to cross the finishing line. It isn't outright victory, and being in front at this point can be more of a pressure than a benefit. A lot is expected once the joust recommences. Few figures express quite so well the hopes and restlessness of football as this false achievement.

In literature, there are only winter champions. Brisk descriptions of team moves and the computable universe of statistics find a place in sports journalism. To enter into the passions through the sports report means taking the facts into account, but only as reference points. The winter champion has earned that position but still isn't fully what it might be; it is composed of the future, and of wishing, and of mere possibility. A virtual victory has an emptiness that dazzles supporters: for them, wishing does help.

Everyone, in his or her way and at whatever point of the year, has his or her winter champion. The lesser, circumstantial fact—this dreaming will wane later on—only goes to show the force of destiny: God may be round, but He hardly ever chooses Necaxa.

THE FINAL PASSION

THOUGH I SHOULDN'T SHOUT about it, defeat suits me. Not that it's precisely a strong point of my own, but rather one of Mexican football. If our happiness were dependent on the scoreboard we'd be professionally sad. Adverse results and so many sitters missed from a few yards out have made us accustomed to enjoying the game without asking too much of Lady Luck.

When someone from the national side scores with a scissor kick—like Manuel Negrete in the 1986 World Cup, or like Raúl Jiménez in the dying seconds of a World Cup qualifier in 2013—the term we use for the action is "another gamer," like it's happened somewhere far removed from where we are in the Estadio Azteca.

Our war cry—*"Sí se puede!"* or "Yes we can!"—is a reminder that our national team almost never has. What Samuel Johnson said of anyone who remarries—that they show "the triumph of hope over experience"—is also a good definition for a Mexico fan's state of mind. His or her faith in the team is based not in reality but in yet-to-be-realized promises. A victory, for us, is a miracle. If it happens we go and celebrate at the Ángel, the statue of the messenger of the gods; if not, we find that the important thing wasn't to win, but just to get together and have a good time.

The passion of a Mexico fan isn't about records, but fantasy. Without quite moving into masochism—we wouldn't deliberately lose—we manage our misfortune with all the resignation of a stoic philosopher. Brazil fans, if their team loses, throw the television out the window. Us, we just order another drink, move into the realm of fantasy, and start to sing, in pride and protest: "But I'm sti-ill the king..."

Maybe we're insane? I don't think so. We're just more interested in the fiesta itself than the thing being celebrated. We're realists, deep down; convinced we'll never get far, we find enjoyment in the here and now, a place that doesn't depend on goals going in. Not that this makes us conformists—not in the slightest. We still get down on our knees and pray in front of Our Lady of the Slender Victory.

My experiences of football from Mexico have made me into a collector of unvictorious situations, which, nonetheless, contain a good deal of grandeur.

In the splendid collection *Memories of San Mamés*, the legendary José Ángel Iribar, a goalkeeper who reached a level of fame similar to that of Lev Yashin, says that the greatest moment in Athletic Bilbao's history was not a goal but a save. Out of the many that littered his own prolific career, he chose not one that he himself was responsible for, but rather one that changed his conception of the game forever.

Telmo Zarra won the Spanish "Pichichi" (the La Liga golden boot) six times, scored an unforgettable goal against England in the Maracanã in the 1950 World Cup, and became the leader in any stats you care to mention related to the scoring of goals. Headers were his specialty. Since England is generally so admired in the Basque country, they came up with the description of Zarra as having "the best head in Europe after Churchill."

He was only ever sent off once—evidence of his unswervingly gentlemanly conduct. And the move that stood out to Iribar had to do with this ethical approach. An obsessive about goals, Zarra nonetheless didn't want to win at any cost. In a match against Málaga, the opposing goalkeeper, Arnau, went down injured, leaving the net wide open. In an act hugely creditable to the game, this deadliest of strikers kicked the ball out of play. The act of mercy put a dent in his many personal records, but won him the admiration of anyone who still believed honesty could exist in the toughest office on Earth—the penalty area. Málaga later awarded him their Insignia de Oro.

In a brilliant piece in the newspaper *Récord*, Miguel Mejía Barón told the following anecdote: "A teammate of mine, Héctor Sanabria, committed a foul that the referee let go.... Don Renato (Cesarini, the Pumas coach in 1963) said to Héctor: 'If the ref isn't going to punish you, I will,' and to my colleague's astonishment—and everyone else's—he subbed him off without sending anyone on to replace him."

In the same article, Mejía Barón recalls the German striker Miroslav Klose, who gave a reminder in 2005 that fair play can still have importance in the beautiful game. In a game for his club side at the time, Werder Bremen, he was tackled by the opposition player Arminia Bielefeld, and the referee, Herbert Fandel, awarded a penalty. Most unusually, Klose went and remonstrated with Fandel, saying it wasn't a foul. Fandel then consulted his linesman and overruled himself. "In all my twenty-five years in the game," he later said, "I've never seen anything like it." Ethics don't tend to prevail in a game where the hugely celebrated Maradona played a prank on destiny itself with his handball against England. Most footballers look to draw fouls, and most will from time to time pretend that they have been fouled. But there are exceptions, and they ought to be remembered.

Star players tend to be egoists who just happen to have fallen into a team game. They see the best moves as the ones that benefit them. For instance, Cristiano Ronaldo can never find it within himself to celebrate a goal that he hasn't had a hand in. His role has to be absolute, and he feels like an extra, superfluous, if someone else scores, even if that someone happens to be on his team.

The vast majority of players feel like this, only they don't dare admit it. So sincere is Cristiano's narcissism that it even blinds us to his other dimensions. One of the downsides of watching matches on the television is the degree to which the camera is a slave to the ball; we only get to see the area immediately around it, making off-the-ball runs invisible, along with players who might not be central in a particular move but want to get involved in the next. CR7 covers a great deal of ground for Real Madrid, just as formidably and with just as much self-sacrifice as a Sergio Ramos; he comes back to defend and takes part in plenty of the less eye-catching attempts to win back the ball. From a purely athletic point of view, he gives an awful lot. But that doesn't extend to emotional generosity; he is self-sacrificing, covers mile after mile of turf, but still only embraces players if the one being congratulated is him.

Many a player would love to be as impudent; they just haven't scored the avalanche of goals that forgives such egoism. Which is why Eric Cantona's statement—that the best thing he did in football wasn't any goal he scored—is so notable. In Ken Loach's excellent film *Looking for Eric*, the striker who so memorably donned Manchester United's red shirt, thinking back through games he was involved in, chooses an *assist* as his perfect moment. What an eloquent way of making the point that football is nothing without one's teammates. Finishing a move is less important than creating one.

You don't need to be a long-suffering Mexico supporter to know that some of the game's greatest moments have occurred away from the goalmouth. Zarra denied himself so as not to humiliate an unfairly stricken goalkeeper. The Bilbao forward was prepared to beat him to be the victor, but not for mere bad fortune.

I've tried to have a perspective that says success often comes to visit, but it isn't the be-all and end-all. Even when considering figures who have been massively, overwhelmingly successful, you find that every achievement is based on an earlier setback.

Mexican parties obey strange laws in the way they unfold: ice is always the first thing to run out, then goes the mineral water, the soft drinks, and lastly the alcohol. The same happens inside the stadium. Take triumph, fame, and glory out of the equation, and it's our passion for the game that remains.

THE SECOND CHILDHOOD

"Genius is merely childhood recaptured," said Baudelaire. The phrase alludes to the origins of creativity, but also to the rose-tinted spectacles through which we view a time that wasn't in fact unadulteratedly happy.

Our early years often seem like an Arcadia, where all was pure pleasure. Nostalgia has its effect: years that might well have been terrible become a green field, growing lusher and more inviting the further we move away from it.

Javier Marías was quite right to term football "the weekly return to childhood." It is an activity in keeping with our early wonderment, the time when there could still be heroes and when all contests resulted in clear winners and losers, with no gray areas. But that doesn't necessarily mean returning to a joyous moment only: "For the child, there is nothing so serious as play." Having fun also signifies some suffering.

The virtues we tend to attribute to being young are less about what happened in reality than a desire to escape the present moment. Returning to childhood voluntarily—via games, via art—permits the adult to take a holiday from his- or herself. This liberating act prompts us, in remembering, to make childhood better than it was, even if it happened to be a dull or painful period in our lives. Being a child is more complex, and far rougher, than we remember.

Suddenly, the bounce of a ball or the indescribable effect of a melody takes us back to an anterior world, the infant instant when miracles were possible and fate was still a thing you could trick. Consciously returning to that condition magnifies and makes a myth of the possibilities of the first childhood. The Olympics, or a book, are deliberately wrought illusions, simulacrums in which we choose to believe—because we are looking for places where magic might still pertain.

Pleasure always has an illusory part, as our desires get mixed up with what might actually be obtained.

Dreams enact curious compensatory mechanisms. While a football supporter dreams of his hat trick in the Maracanã, Pelé's nights are visited by images of missing penalties. That which for the fan is a walk in the park, for the great player is a reality, and all about final scores. Only from the adult perspective can childhood be seen as a place of absolute happiness. In the same way, only from some other destination can we imagine what glory tastes like without having gone through all the efforts required to achieve it.

Sport always takes place in a place midway between the pitch and the imagination. As something is crystallizing, about to come to fruition, the crowd raises its arms. Marías has also discussed the strange body language of fans when a goal goes in. People punching the air and howling—it's hard to think of other circumstances in which the soberest of doctors suddenly unleashes a howl. But why?

The springs activated inside a supporter are bolted deep down—grievances, hopes for reparation, superstition, unfulfilled desires—and they are also distilled the moment the ball rolls over the halfway line. All goals require the mind to be in play simultaneously.

A game's double condition (it is both athletic and mental) becomes triple in these media-saturated times. Certain things "happen" only because they appear on a screen. Zidane's headbutt on Marco Materazzi in the 2006 World Cup wasn't seen on the pitch, because the ball—which everyone follows—was elsewhere; it took the fourth official, watching on a screen, to point out Zidane's misdemeanor. I was in the commentary box and none of us working that night noticed it happen; only when we saw the replay did the incident come into existence.

But TV isn't always as objective as a courtroom. Football is such a subjective business that even cameras are fallible.

One angle might show that a player was onside, and then another that he wasn't. The ghost goal at Wembley featured in many a film without anyone knowing if it went in or not.

Words summon a parallel world. Writing about football means recreating, in another form, that which supporters already know. If it's possible to actually be present at the stadium, who wants a match recounted? This isn't what the words are for. The essence of Pelé or Chicharito "Little Pea" Hernández won't be revealed in any book. It's already there in the minds of the supporters. The rare mystery of words is to put a value and an emotion on what we already know.

When your team scores in the final minute, you make strange expressions, the goal expressions. This lasts a number of seconds. And yet, mysteriously, the discussion of this goal among a group of friends may last a lifetime.

Great moments demand words. Nobody survives a tragedy and stays silent, just as nobody can keep quiet witnessing a goal that really matters.

We watch the game, and we write about football, as a way of returning to childhood, not the one we in fact lived through but the one we ourselves elect. Being young can be hard, full of injustice and anguish. To go back only in our minds is a liberation.

Football improves the childhood we actually had, in the same way that dreams permit us to be different people.

Submerged in this joyful trance, we normal human beings score goals like Pelé. In the meantime, hardworking Edson Arantes dreams of missing altogether.

FATHERS AND SONS

In the run-up to every World Cup, those of us who love the game remind ourselves of the past, hoping to build up emotional credits that might bring miracles our way; visiting our autobiographies becomes a way of courting fortune. Going back through all those inglorious afternoons when we got rained on in the stands, we discover plenty of reasons that things, this time, ought to go well for our national team.

Each fan has his or her own intimate relationship with the game; a crowd in a stadium represents the loudest version of family life. The vast majority of fans are there because once their fathers took them along. Shouting on the group of men wearing certain colors is a mark—the most primitive, perhaps, and the most lasting—of parentage. And for some the adored name of a team is the only thing they inherit.

In my generation, divorce was as unusual as having a parent that lived in Africa. There just weren't any clear codes for fathers when it came to dealing with children that now lived under another roof. The zoo and the cinema (and football) were the go-to options for getting through the weekend. Fascinating as it was to see animals in captivity, it ended up feeling routine; seeing the same caged wolves in the Chapultepec Zoo, ten Sundays in a row, you started to feel you yourself were part of that wearisome pack. The cinema offered more variety, but you couldn't always guarantee the kinds of epics children love to see. Football, on the other hand, meant the renewal of hopes as regularly as the seasons.

My father had been a grudging supporter of Asturias. When the University side, Pumas, were promoted to the first division, he backed them with a trade union-like solidarity. He made the young me feel that goals flooded him with excitement—that he enjoyed the game as much as I did. He missed Barcelona, the city where he was born, and talked about the blaugrana with the fevered sense of belonging that only those in exile ever experience. When I finished high school and set off on some travels for six months, he would write to me every Monday, always including a newspaper cutting of the league table.

The stands were, for him, an extension of the classroom. Surrounded by the salted-pepita eaters, and men chewing on pork rinds, he was still the same ethics professor as at work. If anyone nearby insulted the opposition, he'd tell them off, and no one ever dared argue with his reasoning: "That's no way to treat a guest!" he'd say.

He once wrote a piece about the 1974 World Cup in Germany for Julio Scherer's *Excélsior*, arguing that football, in its sphere of pure play, acted as a compensatory mechanism for political realities. It was the only place where Haiti had a chance of being better than Italy.

Once I grew old enough to go to matches on my own, my father stopped going. The peculiar emotions I experience when watching a match, however, can only be explained by the fact that that was where he had been present in my childhood.

There are countless similar cases. In his novel *Dark Light*, the Chilean writer Nicolás Vidal describes the relationship between a father and son via experiences they have inside stadiums. And other eminent football evangelists (I'm thinking about the Argentine Eduardo Sacheri and the Chilean Francisco Mouat) have underlined the importance of sharing with their sons the triumphs of Independiente and Universidad de Chile.

Martín Caparrós is one of the writers to have best tackled the subject. "My son was born in 1991," he writes in *Boquita*, up until which time, say if I were planning a trip to China, my main worry wouldn't be whether I was going to miss the match on the weekend. Until Juan came along. Then, for some reason, I realized how important it seemed that he become a Boca Junior supporter. It was an interesting thought: I imagined that if it became our custom to watch Boca together, then at some point, once he was old enough to have far more interesting things to do than to hang out with his old man, Boca might be something that held us together, or would give us, at least, the chance to spend a bit of time in the same place. Perhaps the formulation wasn't quite so exact, but it was along these lines. I later found out that other people had had the same idea—as in, millions of other people. And this is how I view anything in culture—as offering a shared space.

Years later, Caparrós was on his way to the Bombonera, his son Juan alongside him, when the singer Iván Noble came on the radio. Noble had just had a son himself, and had read *Boquita*, and quoted the above passage. Juan Caparrós was twenty-three now, and was still sharing with his father the common space of being a Boca fan.

All of which leads me to confess a personal emotional defeat: my own son Juan Pablo, a very good goalkeeper, nonetheless doesn't really care for football. When I pointed this out to Caparrós, he had the wisdom to say that "sharing football can also mean you don't share anything else." He didn't mean himself, but the vast numbers of fathers who *only* talk to their sons when their team is playing.

A stadium is a good place to have your father there. The rest of the world is a good place to have your son there.

LOVE FOR THE SHIRT?

The inventiveness of nature means we wouldn't even be surprised now to see a Dalmatian with stripes or a zebra with spots. There's no end to the wildness of beasts.

In man's zeal for opposing nature's plan, the designer pet trend has taken off—fish that light up in the dark, hypoallergenic cats. Luckily these alterations haven't yet moved into the realm of commerce. The Japanese scientist is yet to be born with the ability to create puppies with Toyota ads for markings.

What an animal looks like depends on its genetic code (whether that be natural or engineered), the only exception being our species, which makes underpants out of vine leaves and has evolved so that personality is now the thing that defines a person's character.

The football shirt as an identity marker and a sign of belonging came about in the days when every player—or their poor mother—still had to wash their own. At the time no one thought it would come to have any value other than as a symbol; players didn't get a wage, and fans just used the black strip on the shirts of one team, and the white and red stripes on the other, to distinguish the players.

In those early days, footballers stuck around for a long time—long like Russian novels. They'd prove themselves by coming up through the ranks of the team they supported—almost always their local team—then sign a contract for life, in exchange for a pair of boots or, if they were lucky, a little bit of money, and set their sights no further ahead than the opposition goal.

The invention of transfers generated a powerful emotional enigma: Can a player really support a team just because they happened to pay some money for him? In the professional era, with players always aware that they might move elsewhere, no one expects them to sleep in their kit anymore or to drench it in tears after a defeat.

A "love for the shirt" began as something literal (a connection with a single, lovingly darned item of clothing) before becoming a synonym, a way of referring to the respect for the shirt that is underwritten by a work-for-hire arrangement. A professional doesn't have to be a fan of his team to honor it.

Up until the 1970s, football etiquette was severely codified: tugging someone's shirt was a shameful thing to do. Kits were so fitted they were almost skintight, so if you were going to impede an opponent you had to pinch and scratch them, too. The other thing was the limitation to squad numbers: 1 to 11 covered the players on the pitch, and all the rest were the substitutes. The numbers corresponded not only with a position but with something moral. "I play ten," a player would say, and if they were anyone but Pelé would thereby reveal their overweening hubris. Or, "I needed a ten and they bought me a five," a manager would complain. The shirt therefore held a geographical value, indicating *where* on the pitch you'd go to express yourself.

Of Johan Cruyff's many extravagances, for example, his decision to wear the number 14 was not inconsiderable.

Midway through the 1970s, Don Revie, the Leeds United manager, had the idea of getting a clothes brand to make the team shirts, and then putting them in the shops. There was nothing particularly extravagant about a shirtmaker wanting to promote itself, but soon other companies were getting in on the act. In 1978 the carmaker Saab began sponsoring Derby County, and in 1979 the red shirt of Liverpool saw a Japanese name splashed across it: Hitachi.

The rest is history, as footballers have become walking advertisements—not dissimilar to the men who used to go around wearing sandwich boards.

At first British television refused to air these marketing strategies, since it stood to gain nothing. Teams signed an agreement not to wear shirts with these commercial stains on them for any televised matches. In 1983, the BBC finally agreed to broadcast matches with players wearing advertising, at which point the prices for getting your company onto the chests of players skyrocketed.

"The style is the man himself," wrote Buffon (not the Italian goalkeeper but the eighteenth-century French writer, Georges-Louis Leclerc, Comte de Buffon). The aphorism has been widely used to praise the work of tailors, but fabrics in themselves can't turn a profit. In the 1980s, it became the norm to denigrate football shirts in three ways: they became another hoarding for advertising, they got baggier, and you could have any number you liked on the back. An iconography that had come together over the course of a hundred years suddenly lost its main sense. A team's colors became a remote cause, allowing yogurt companies to promote their wares.

Behind these changes lies a very well-known fact: football is the most money-spinning form of passion on the planet. Félix Fernández, an ex-goalkeeper-turned-commentator, informs us that no fewer than 270 million people are connected with the sport worldwide.

So an emblem of identity has become a business platform. Official merchandise can be more profitable than goals. This is a world in which transfer outlays are largely canceled out by the shirts sold with X player's name on the back. It's such big business that the name of one of these demigods itself takes on all the power of a brand. In Real Madrid's official club shop, the blue shirt with number 1 on the back costs more if you get "Casillas" printed on it, too.

We live on a fickle planet in which companies vary from country to country. Barcelona lasted until the end of the twentieth century without allowing advertising on their shirt. When they first gave in to the temptation, they went for a social cause and had UNICEF on the chest, as well as a small logo for TV3, the Catalan TV station, on the sleeve.

"I can resist everything except temptation," said Oscar Wilde. Under Joan Laporta, Barca stayed faithful to UNICEF, but with the arrival of Sandro Rosell as director, the Qatar Foundation became the club sponsor. From infants to petroleum: a neat metaphor for the salability of fans' connections with their club.

Mexican teams sully their shirts with a mélange of products for hyperactive consumers: in no more than twelve inches of fabric you are encouraged to drink milk, book a flight, open a bank account, and pick up the phone.

You only need look at the Mexico national strip to know that football is not well managed. Is it really possible for a player to identify with a shirt that is also a sales catalog? To make matters worse, being a player in the country of the eagle and serpent means constantly putting on new shirts. In a league where the big money lies in transfers and the attendant commissions rather than in winning titles, the player becomes a nomad, constantly moving on. "Love is eternal, as long as it lasts," wrote Vinícius de Moraes. Can we really expect a player to profess eternal love for the duration of his contract?

A place of untold abuses and speculation, Mexican football functions by making a quick buck. As an organization it's exceedingly backward, making club owners and executives rich while preventing constancy from players.

This being the case, it wouldn't be fair to ask for loyalty from players who themselves do not receive it.

In our current age, fidelity has become the luxury of millionaires: Paolo Maldini was a symbol for Milan in the way Totti was for Roma or Buffon for Juventus. They're unusual in having, at some point, declared themselves not for sale. As for managers, there have been some exceptional cases, like that of Guy Roux, who was in charge of Auxerre in France for no less than forty-four years. According to Alberto Lati, this unrepent-antly settled man did tire after working with the same team for almost half a century. He retired, but only to feel the flutter of nostalgia and go back into management a couple of years later with a different team. It wasn't the same; after so many loyal years, the change of scenery felt like a betrayal.

If footballers reject the salary hike of signing for a side owned by a ruble-happy Russian magnate, it's only because they've already amassed a sufficient fortune and can afford not to. Nowadays, to support the team you play for you either need to be starting your first game for the club or have special powers.

Mexicans, on the other hand, increasingly need to call on their powers of self-deception. Good on you if you're able to discern your team's colors under all those ads! This power of mental transfiguration means that, even in these strange times, fans' love for the shirt hasn't disappeared at all.

Some clubs try to emphasize the significance of the shirt by some dramatic gesture. Like Schalke 04, who cling on to their sense of identity in the massively well-off Bundesliga. In his book *Latitudes*, Alberto Lati talks about new signings being presented to the media at the bottom of a coal mine, as a way of recalling the "worker's tradition of the city and the humble values the players are expected to defend." It isn't all about the money in football—just *nearly* all.

Every Monday, the strip is taken to the laundry. And long-suffering fans will be forgiven for hoping they might come back one day with all the advertising washed off.

EXTREME ATTACHMENT:
REASONS TO COMMIT SUICIDE TWICE

So football is life's predictable part. We don't know if we'll find time to go to the dentist or do the week's shopping, but one thing's certain: we plan enough to know where we're going to watch the Champions League final.

When there aren't any matches to watch, we talk about football, or at least we talk about astronomical transfers. There's less action during the summer, but there's always some FIFA embezzlement or other to discuss, or a national team going out bingeing, or Clenbuterol in the urine of a player. Hardly epic themes, but they enable the conversation to continue.

The neuropsychiatrist Jesús Ramírez-Bermúdez's book *A Brief Clinical Dictionary of the Soul* analyzes clinical histories with the same narrative pulse as Oliver Sacks. It includes reference to D.H., a young salesperson from England who gets knocked over in a car accident. D.H.'s head hits the pavement and though his skull isn't fractured, he's left with an injury that creates a strange alteration. The world seems to him not only changed, but suspicious. D.H. knows, as we all do, that fate is capricious, and that when you forget your umbrella, the skies open. As a way of overcoming the inconstancy of this world, he took refuge in football, this impassioned form of repetitiveness: Man Utd vs. Man City will *always* be a nail-biter, and we'll *never* know who was greater, Pelé or Maradona.

A few days after his accident, D.H. noticed that his wife, the houses around where he lived, and the news, too, had all undergone certain changes. It was the end of summer 2004 and the U.S. president, George Bush, was saying strange things—stranger and stranger. How to recover his old confidence in the universe?

The English patient acted with the kind of determination that transcends cultures, creating a fellowship between the Spanish *forofo* and the Italian *tifoso*, the Argentine *hincha* and the Mexican *aficionado*. He wanted to find out the truth: that is, he started checking the results page.

But then, even stranger news: Greece had won the European Championship, and Australia had qualified for the World Cup. Now reality had become illogical. "I always thought," he said in his exasperated testimony, "that the only real thing on the TV was football... Now the news is all so absurd. Greece, champion of Europe? Australia in the World Cup? Christ, these were more unbelievable than anything. That was why I tried to kill myself those two times. I tried to hang myself in the bathroom at home. But both times I messed it up."

D.H. was suffering from Cotard's syndrome, named after the French doctor Jules Cotard, who discovered the "delirium of negation." Sufferers find themselves in a place full of uncertainty: they deny their name, the existence of their body and of their emotions. The only thing D.H. believed was football. Then Greece not only got to a final but also won.

After failing to kill himself, he came to think that his punishment was eternity, a hell in which even oblivion and death had ceased to exist. Curiously, the thing he was most affected by wasn't the distortion his world had undergone, but authentic, genuine facts—featured in the sports section. Immersed in madness, he was on the verge of dying from reality.

D.H.'s suffering is an extreme illustration of the tensions most everyday fans experience. Football gives a structure to our year, and means we can change our fate into something that is, to a greater or lesser degree, predictable: we can decide where we'll watch the Champions League Final, if not necessarily what the result will mean for us.

THE ART OF SHOUTING

Football is a good excuse to make a lot of noise. The same person whose wife reproaches him—"Why don't you talk? Aren't you listening?"—grabs the keys and goes to the match to shout his lungs off.

A goal is an excuse to lose your composure. At this moment it becomes not only logical but also desirable for your neighbor to howl with delight.

To consummate this act, the lungs are required, the throat, the tonsils, and even the hairs on the back of one's neck. A cry only becomes truly celebratory if the mind goes on holiday, letting the body do the rest.

In Spanish football vocabulary, there's a word that is equally essential to the upkeep of the football as to screaming with unbridled delight: hincha, which is Spanish both for "fan" and "inflate."

Many years ago I heard the great radio commentator Víctor Hugo Morales talk about the Uruguayan origins of the word: it was firstly used to describe the boy on the side of the pitch who blew up the balls. How utterly logical for celebrations, and footballs, to be seen as blowing up in the same way: passion for the game as pneumatic.

So Uruguay left the Spanish-speaking world a word for uproar and celebration, but also the capacity to leave stadiums in complete silence, especially on July 16. On that day in 1950, the Uruguayan national team beat Brazil in the World Cup Final, and in 2011 they beat Argentina in the Copa America Final. When a hush falls over the stands, it means that no matter who's playing at home, so is silence.

The Uruguayans perfected the art of shouting for themselves and silencing others, and have been widely imitated, if never credited. In 2009 I went to a match in Kyoto, with the home team playing their regional clásico against Osaka. I found out in that small stadium that for the Japanese, even enthusiasm is subject to courteousness: the home and away fans would take turns shouting for their teams.

The oddest thing was hearing them imitate Argentine anthems—they'd taken classes in yelling from the fans in Buenos Aires. That which at the Boca stadium would have been a jungle of noise was there sculpted down into a sound-bonsai.

Fans can be divided into two kinds: there are the materialists, who keep an eye on the scoreboard to see whether their hopes are being pumped up or deflated, and there are the romantics, who don't need such evidence in order to shout their team on. And it is only the second group that deserves the name hinchas. Those who came up with the term began their cries in the times when Uruguay was the best team in the world, but they carried on even as their team's star waned, which just goes to show that in football devotion itself is enough to sustain devotion.

WHY DO FOOTBALLERS SPIT?: A PUNCTUATION ISSUE

There was a time when the act of spitting was socially recognized. When I was a child, lawyers' offices and doctors' waiting rooms always had something in the corner: a metal spittoon. Humankind presumably faces the same challenges today as to what to do with saliva, and yet public vessels for your sputum have disappeared.

Football is the place where people professionally unloose phlegm. At the end of a match, the camera zooms in on the protagonists. We see them raise their eyes skyward, up to where their grandparents reside, along with their hopes to be more accurate in front of goal; then we see a shake of the head, as though coming so agonizingly close left them with water in their eardrums; finally, we see them spit on the ground.

Why does this happen? In tennis, players touch their racket strings as a way of concentrating. The same cannot be said of the relationship between a football player and his spit; no one plays any better having rid his mouth of a bit of dribble. Rather it is a way of discharging nervousness, and frustration, too. Gobbing is the only tranquilizer that works when a player has been sent off. And a gesture deemed reprehensible in any other situation doesn't matter here, in view of millions of people.

All language requires punctuation. Football has more than its fair share of exclamation marks (a goal being scored, a player openly cheating, the miraculous sliding tackle) and ellipses (a player rolling around after being fouled, a ball being cleared into Row Z, a pass into space with no one to collect it).

Certain geniuses of the game, like Butragueño and Valderrama, are able to slow the ball down, putting the clock in parentheses; others, like Xavi and Andrés Iniesta, pile up comma after comma to create serial subordinate clauses. Romário was one of the few equally able to deploy full stop and comma, with that wonderful shot of his and the ability to perfectly weight a pass.

Defenders and strikers alike love a paragraph break. Street players, for whom it's just as important to get past your opponent as it is to finish off a move, are like the Spanish opening question marks (the clause containing a question not only ends with a question mark, but begins with an initial, upside-down one: ¿)—they don't necessarily ask the whole question. Insulting your opposite number and complaints to the referee are the equivalents of speech marks.

What about the "..." that announces something is about to happen? That's in a player's shout. The most consistently overused punctuation mark, in the way it announces a surprise that doesn't always come off, is used both crudely and effectively. No one ever spits when they are in motion or after they have scored a goal (a culmination like that needs no haven of tranquility). It is only the compulsory transitions that require this act; the move or shot or pass failed to come off, but life goes on. And it doesn't mean a player is sad or annoyed either, but that he is venting something, and thereby warning everyone that things aren't over: a colon.

Good moves in football add up to 5 percent of a match. The rest is things not going to plan, mistakes, and these are the times in which minds turn to what is about to happen—when throats get a rest, in other words.

Certain spits have become infamous. Frank Rijkaard, cool-headed as a player, and endowed with a Franciscan patience as a manager, made a grave error of punctuation. In a match at Italia '90, he wanted to put Rudi Völler in speech marks, but as he didn't speak German, he unleashed a despicable gob of phlegm. The perplexity of the striker was unforgettable, the way he reacted like a pirate who had been splattered with a jellyfish.

No human life is untouched by tics: some people fiddle with an earlobe, some play with their keys. As a territory of uncertainty, football is a place where heroes fail almost constantly before finding their faith again, gearing themselves up to try something different—though not before they have spat on the turf.

ETERNITY PASSES QUICKLY

When childhood comes to an end, human beings are stupefied to discover that toys are no longer any use, and that they're going to die one day. To make up for the simultaneous loss of magical objects and eternal life, a talisman was fashioned.

Obviously I am talking about the football.

The history of the round toy is a very long one. In 2012 I went and saw the incredibly tall ruins at Toniná, in the Mexican state of Chiapas. The archaeologist Juan Yadeun, who is in charge of the area, showed me a frieze that depicted a football made from the head of a conquered opponent. "Centuries before Dunlop vulcanized the oilcloth," he told me, "the Maya already knew how to do it." In his view, the pitch that most resembles the one in *Popol-Vuh* is this one in Toniná.

Metaphors for duality, the sacred games of the pre-Hispanic peoples were stagings of the struggle between day and night, life and death, paradise and the underworld. The oilcloth ball was, in and of itself, a sign of metamorphosis: made from ashes, it represented resurrection—the cosmic wheel, on which destruction feeds future energies. A death breathed new life.

Balls that were bouncing around and being kicked thousands of years ago are with us still. The archaeological site of Cantona, in the state of Pueblo, has more than twenty pitches, and the one in Tajín, Veracruz, features the strangest of all: at the heart of the city stood a scale model of a game, which wasn't used for sporting purposes but as a form of prayer—an altar to football.

In the West, immortality was also sought in a round ball. As the etymology of *pelota* ("ball" in Spanish) suggests, a ball was originally made of hair (*pelo*), which is the only body part, apart from the nails, that appears to continue growing after death.

In his wonderful novel *Sudden Death*, Álvaro Enrigue discusses the singular history of four tennis balls made from Anne Boleyn's red hair after she was executed, and reflects on the handiwork of the hereafter: "not everyone was willing to produce an object that took its life from the only part of a dead body that doesn't rot."* Long before science fiction and zombie movies, balls were already allowing the dead to live on.

Sudden Death features a tennis match between Francisco de Quevedo and Caravaggio. According to the historical records, it's not entirely unfeasible that the encounter took place. Both artists were in Rome at the same time, both were familiar with tennis (or its antecedent), and both had competitive—not to mention murderous—tendencies. One of Quevedo's most well-known phrases could just as easily be applied to a football: "Naught but the wave—a fugitive—remains."† The ball gave a person's ashes a life after death. For its part, the ball of Renaissance times stands as a reminder that though the organism corrupts, the hair "remains."

Footballs were originally made of stitched leather and had to be handled as lightly as a puppy. They had to be inflated, smeared with fat, and you couldn't get them wet (if it was rainy for a match, heading the ball meant an automatic migraine). As the writer Vicente Verdú has pointed out, with the arrival of the white, plastic ball, football lost its agricultural tone; the pitch, which until then resembled a field to be tilled, began to be more like a residential garden.

---

*   From the translation by Natasha Wimmer.

†   From the translation by Felicia Hemans.

At every World Cup, players have the additional challenge of adjusting to a new ball. In South Africa 2010, the Jabulani—which means "jubilation" in Zulu—was as slippery as a trout in keepers' hands, and some forwards kicked it as though they were quoting Vicente Huidobro, who sought to "extinguish a cockerel as one puts out a fire." Every four years, it's as though the new ball needs to be tamed, not controlled.

The history of the football has been dictated by the light. In matches played at night, the floodlights make the grass sparkle, and make the football seem like a big muddy stain. Also, stadiums grew in size, and the tanned leather, erred in its discreetness, came to seem out of place.

Proof that humans are strange: to make the ball stand out more, at times it has been painted black. Maybe it was a pool fan, enamored of the eight ball, who came up with the idea. This improvement meant free eye tests for all, until some genius discovered that white stood out in the dark.

The color of the ball accelerated the trend that was leading toward the replacement of leather by plastics, and football's last contact with farming was severed.

Before that, balls were alive in a peculiar way. Sometimes they'd have been re-stitched, and some kicks would loosen the stitches, and then they'd have to be pumped up again.

As the game industrialized, the balls previously used were not substituted for with an equivalent, but an altogether new object: the fast-moving ball, a ultra-light projectile in place of the bladders stuffed with hairs. At the end of every match, Alfredo di Stéfano used to pick up the ball and thank it, with the same affection with which you might caress your grandmother's wrinkled cheek. Would he have done the same with a synthetic ball? Surely not.

The alchemists at Adidas *could* make heavier balls, but it would make no sense. Football has become a much faster sport alongside the process of the ball itself becoming lighter.

When North Korea beat Italy in the 1966 World Cup, I remember noticing the way their players ran all the time. Until then, football was a sport in which only mediocre players had to be in a hurry. In his playing days, the Argentine César Luis Menotti was upbraided by a friend for not chasing a pass, and his response was indicative of the time: "As well as playing, I have to run?" he said.

It's impossible to know if football became quicker due to the changes to the ball, or the ball adapted to ever-faster players. What's not in question is that doctors became all the more central in the game, and the pharmaceutical industry began coming up with energy pills and antioxidant lozenges.

What's fabulous about this story is that it hasn't come to an end. Some people even try to liberate the ball from its engagement with footballers. The developers are as competitive as José Mourinho, and they'll never find the ideal circumference. This is added to, of course, by having to constantly provide new products to sell. At the beginning of every competition, thousands of balls are sent to the Siberia of toys to make way for the season's new model.

Perhaps because jubilation is no easy thing to grasp, the Jabulani was more problematic than anyone expected and became a ready-made, spherical excuse for keepers who spilled shots.

The Brazuca, the official match ball at Brazil 2014, was made from the subtle polyurethanes and latexes invented in Germany. This doesn't make it exempt from superstitions: its color scheme is based on Brazil's popular "Senhor do Bonfim" wish ribbons.

Kicked around with profane persistence, the balls are the symbol of a species—us—which, as it moves into adulthood, leaves aside its toys and acknowledges death.

Like so many other objects that are full of meaning, its message is ironic. Evasive and liable to shift unpredictably, it is a reminder that eternity passes quickly.

WHEN A GOAL IS
MORE THAN A GOAL

THE LONGEST GOAL IN THE WORLD

There is a distant Chinese fable that points to the world's fragile interconnectedness. A tiny object, thrown into the Yellow Sea, can affect faraway beaches. In a secret and inextricable way, everything is everything.

Unexpected messages are carried on the tides, from one side of the ocean to the other. The city of Guerrero Negro in Baja California Sur takes its name from a ship that ran aground there; in cetacean waters, the Black Warrior ended its days like a beached whale. A local restaurant named Malarrimo has a net on the wall bearing torpedoes, lamps, and other objects that have washed up on the nearby shore. Storms are like a slow postal service; sooner or later objects thrown into the sea will end up in some post box or other.

On March 11, 2011, a force-nine earthquake hit the coasts of Japan and a tsunami flipped over cars and houses inland.

Fourteen months later, five million metric tons of scrap metal were still being carried along by the tides, in the direction of the Americas. What we have here is a metaphor for memory: not everything we experience is retained, and not all memories are instantly accessible, as some take a while to surface. The loose pieces grabbed by Japan were assimilated into this loose mosaic of a country before ending up in hands that never expected to receive them.

David Baxter grew up amongst the ice and rocks of Middleton Island, Alaska. He works in the radar station. In the afternoons and evenings, peeling his eyes away from the screen and its panoply of vibrating lights, the world strikes him as being like a second radar on which he has to impose some order. On weekends he relaxes by going beachcombing. It's a treeless landscape. A wide, windswept landscape with nothing to obstruct the view. The only place you're going to find anything is in the sand.

Baxter is skillful at uncovering the remains brought in by the sea, but he never expected to be a witness to the longest goal in the world. One evening, a ball rolled onto the beach.

The inhabitants of Middletown know well the swift movements of the fox and the underwater evasiveness of the seal, and Baxter quickly trapped the ball. He was particularly interested to see that the ball had Japanese script on it. A message from shipwreck survivors? Perhaps the signs joined together in some way. Something must have sunk, in some faraway place, for the ball to pitch up here.

Perhaps chance is just another name for deliberation, and accidents happen so as to make fate *seem* spontaneous. If not, how to explain the fact that the man who found the ball was married to a Japanese woman?

Yumi Baxter deciphered the writing that same evening. The script spoke not of a shipwreck but of a country. The ball had floated all the way from Japan: a three-thousand-mile journey. It had taken thirteen months to arrive. It turned out to belong to Misaki Murakami, a sixteen-year-old schoolboy whose home had been washed away by the tsunami.

Five years earlier, Misaki had moved schools, and his friends had written their names on his football to prevent him from forgetting them. The ball was a memory storage unit. And now it was in the hands of a radar controller.

You only need a few details to start concocting a story: some children who wanted their schoolmate to remember them; a love of football; the loss of a home; the movements of the oceans; a man who felt the need to comb beaches, looking for signs in the sand.

Baxter decided to travel to Japan to return the ball. Maybe it was a date destiny had already decided on. A ball's *raison d'être* is to enter a goal; things presuppose the effect they will have. As it was in the Chinese fable, a butterfly flapping its wings has the capacity to alter the course of someone's life half a world away. All motion, faint as it may be, has consequences.

The ultimate potential of anything is magic, which can change reality in inexplicable ways. Though that isn't to say logic doesn't govern it. "Magic is the coronation or the nightmare of the causal, not its contradiction," wrote Borges.

The Japanese ball had that rare touch of magic. Nineteen thousand people died in the country best equipped for such a disaster. Nature, once more, showed itself to be the inviolable limit of all things. And yet the ball floated out across the waters, like an omen, a suggestion of what was to come in later years.

At some point the planet will vanish into dust and residue, but one thing eludes nature. Not everything is tangible: things are also symbols. That was the way the Chinese fabulist saw it when he wrote that everything is everything, as did the unknown originator of a spherical object that generates hopes and dreams as it bounces around, the children that wrote on it, turning it into something that stores memory, the teenager who lost his home but not the memories of what happened in it, and the radar controller who gathered signs from very far away.

The ball went back to Japan, but that might not have been the end of its journey. Maybe other dates have been set for it.

Stadiums exist so that magic can be played with. The world, so that it can live.

THE GOAL THAT HAPPENED TWICE

Ghost goals are a common challenge to the imagination. Did it go in, or did it hit the line and bounce out? In cases where it isn't clear, it's personal preference that decides what the eye is too weak to see.

On April 18, 2007, Lionel Messi came up with an entirely new kind of ghost goal, scoring a carbon copy of a past goal that had already gone down as unique, impossible to repeat. Twenty-one years after Maradona left half a dozen Englishmen on their backsides for his goal at Mexico '86, the Flea created an exact replica against Spanish club side Getafe. Both moves occurred in the same parts of the pitch, both lasted eleven seconds, and both were executed by excessively brilliant Argentines.

Messi's goal prompts reflection on the strange art of the copyist. The Argentine writer Juan Sasturain compared the forward with Pierre Menard, the Borges character who dedicated his life to creating a line-for-line identical copy of *Don Quixote*. With supreme irony, Borges creates this fool who nonetheless has a great turn: the copy is to be identical, but will exist in a different era, forcing its readership to read "his" *Quixote* not as a work from the 1600s, but in contemporary terms. Context is all in art. In the story, Borges makes fun of critics' tendency to overinterpret, but at the same time puts forward the possibility that someone will be original as the *second author* of a work. Such was the case with Marcel Duchamp and Leonardo's *Mona Lisa*, when the former painted a mustache onto the classic image, only to erase it, so that what was left was a "shaved" *Mona Lisa*.

Messi's goal expresses—simply and conclusively—just how creative an imitator can be; it was a marvel, which, at the same time, no one even considered calling original. "In these days of mechanized football," writes Sasturain,

> of preconceived moves and their obedient executors, it's not unusual to see a great many similar goals—there's an infinite amount of examples with carbon-copy circumstances and performances—the extraordinary thing here,

precisely, is that the thing being magically repeated was, by definition, unrepeatable and exceptional: the greatest goal in the history of the game. Messi's goal was neither better nor worse but, more unsettlingly, *the same*. He did not score a similar goal, he did not copy or imitate or translate: simply, incredibly, he scored it again.

Messi, *à la* Pierre Menard, was the scorer of a masterpiece that already existed.

Until then, Maradona's goal had, in an almost abusive way, been the greatest goal ever. It had set him apart in the history of World Cups. Never before or since has a player been so central to a team; Maradona gave the impression in 1986 that he just needed to be given the ball to elevate his team to world champions. "El Negro" Enrique, who gave him the ball in midfield, summarized perfectly their "Diego dependence": "See that assist I laid on for you?" was his mischievous comment afterward. That bog-standard pass in the middle of the pitch had, in effect, been an assist.

Football is a machine for myths, and that legitimate goal by Maradona was preceded by one he scored with his hand, which he later dubbed "the hand of God." Diego left his mark on the game with all the duality or duplicity of his talent; in 1986, for ninety summer minutes against England, he was both Jekyll and Hyde.

Messi's version of the goal, in which another extravagantly talented player left half a team dizzy in his wake, was unsettling in the same way a miracle is unsettling: the best goal is two goals. Though Diego's was more significant because of the World Cup setting, Messi reproduced its brilliance instant by instant, making it in no way a lesser goal, containing everything required of a true imitator, a true ghost.

Jorge Valdano pointed out that the astonishing thing wasn't merely Messi's avid repetition, but that destiny should present him with such an identical obstacle course. Twenty-one years on, a group of defenders made the same mistakes, in the same places on the pitch, with all the meticulousness of creatures hypnotized in the name of a great cause. No one came in and simply wiped the genius out.

Anything extraordinary awakens suspicions in this imperfect world of ours, and many people point out that both goals could have been prevented with a little bit of brute force. But it's such a lame argument—it's as though the argument itself had suffered a heavy tackle. It would have needed a *lucha libre*-esque clothesline to stop the sashaying sprints of those escape artists, so embarrassing, so blush-inducing, that red faces would have been the only outcome—not to mention a red card.

The notable difference between the goals is that Maradona scored with his left foot and Messi with his right. The second was more amazing for also being a mirror. For an eleven-second stretch, driven on by the goal-scoring impulse, Leo couldn't have known he was imitating the intricacies of Diego's effort; he acted with the spontaneity of a doppelgänger, making the other the same. When he slotted the ball home, he was scoring twice, once in the Camp Nou net, and once in the memory of the fans previously dazzled by Maradona's effort.

1986, 2007. These are the dates. What is strange, and fascinating, is that neither goal is lessened by the comparison. The first in a sense grows more potent as it takes on the status of a prophecy—for the goal to come—and the one that came after is also more powerful for being a classical allusion.

In the world of action, there's no such thing as plagiarism or copyright. Messi's goal can only be seen as a virtuoso effort. It transformed football into an unquantifiable activity, one in which the unique can happen twice.

THE GOALS PELÉ DIDN'T SCORE

Football is this insane activity in which it can actually be dangerous to score certain goals. There was a thirty-year period when it did you no good to be the first to score in the final of a World Cup.

It all began in the Uruguayan capital, Montevideo, in the Estadio Centenario, on July, 30, 1930. The hosts were to face their archrivals Argentina. The crowd poured in eight hours before kickoff, and the referee demanded that a boat be readied in the port for him, in case he had to make a quick getaway after blowing the final whistle.

The final's first goal was scored by an Argentine with a perfect name for the occasion: Pablo Dorado—or Pablo "Golden."

The visitors celebrated their lead with great optimism, but unbeknownst to them they were actually inaugurating a curse. From that day on, for a long time, the team that scored first in the final would always end up coming in second. Uruguay came through 4–2, the opener acting on them like a tonic, kick-starting their performance. And then, every four years, the gods of the game showed how jealous and vengeful they were, spurning the more ambitious side, the one to land the first blow, rewarding whoever began the match on the wrong foot.

The bad luck was still in effect in 1970. In the interim, any team that came out of the blocks too quickly had been punished every time.

My father took me to Brazil vs. Italy. As we were making our way to the Estadio Azteca, he reeled off an axiom of the game: "Whoever scores first, loses." With great defiance, Pelé put Brazil in front with a magical header. I can remember seeing Gérson standing in midfield with his hands pressed together in prayer. Thanking the Lord or pleading for mercy?

Football is easily strange enough for the workaday Italy side to have benefited from the poison goal. Boninsegna leveled the score soon after. A forty-year accumulation of superstition meant that the Azzurri were, in that moment, favorites. But as it turned out, as Pier Paolo Pasolini has written, Brazil came up with football poetry, far superior to the Italian prose. The triumph of Pelé's team was resounding, with a final score of 4–1, the Jules Rimet going back to Brazil, and the curse of the first goal vanquished.

How could Pelé have known that by opening the scoring he wasn't jeopardizing his team's chances? He was supported by a curious arithmetic. It was a World Cup that would also be remembered for the goals he didn't score. In a way the wonderful header he put past Enrico Albertosi was merely compensation for others, more wonderful still, that he had *nearly* scored in the same competition.

In the match against Czechoslovakia, he picked up the ball on the halfway line and spotted the goalkeeper, Ivo Viktor, a long way off his line. The parabola of Pelé's shot, both gentle and dangerous, for a number of seconds made it the most beautiful goal ever scored in a World Cup, until it went just wide.

And then against Uruguay he was through on goal, one-on-one with the legendary keeper Ladislao Mazurkiewicz, and instead of controlling the ball or taking a shot, he let it roll past him—a feint that wrong-footed the keeper, who had no way of deciphering this non-move. The King followed the ball he'd laid on for himself without having touched it: the strangest assist in the history of the game. The number 10 caught up with the ball in an awkward position. And even so, he shot, and nearly scored.

And what about his best effort against England? As the sun beat down in Guadalajara, he sent a jackhammer of a downwards header that bounced on the goal line, doing everything one demigod can do to overcome another, but Churchill's nation is not to be beaten from the air, and Gordon Banks pulled off the greatest save of his life, twisting himself over and back and palming the ball wide.

If these three goals had gone in, they would have been less memorable. It was their very impossibility that etched them in memory.

From that day in 1930 when an anxious referee called for a boat on which to make his getaway, superstition dictated you ought not to score first. To overturn the curse, Edson Arantes do Nascimento had to pay with a strange trio of non-goals. He won the World Cup in 1970, but more significantly demonstrated that while football is all about goals, most especially it is about the hope that they might occur.

GOAL FORGIVEN

In 1942, during the Nazi occupation of Kiev, the old members of the local football team, Dynamo Kiev, were working in State Bakery Number 3.

In the summer, a miracle occurred of the kind that only the sun can bestow on cold countries: football began again. The communist bakers set up a team called "Start." They put several goals past a team of Ukrainian compatriots, before similarly trouncing a team from Hungary.

On July 28, Stalin proclaimed Order 227, which he summed up in five words: "Not a single backward step." Tension was mounting in Kiev when the Start side took on a team from Germany, the Flakelf eleven.

The Ukrainians obeyed Order 227, winning 5–1. Though the prisoners did nothing to break any rules, they'd succeeded in wounding Germanic pride.

Sport was one of the most important axes on which Nazi ideology turned. In 1936, when Germany lost to Norway at the Berlin Olympics, Goebbels wrote the following in his diary: "A hundred thousand people drifted away from the stadium in a state of depression. Winning at sport could be just as important to us as taking some town or other to the east." Flakelf demanded revenge.

The second match took place on August 9. The referee was a member of the SS, and the German team received reinforcements (not the greatest players of all time, but some very fit fighter pilots, at least).

The referee visited the Ukrainian changing rooms before the match, and told them they had to do a Nazi salute as they came out on the pitch. When the players had a discussion about what to do, it led to the usual Leftist non-conclusion—disagreement and quarreling. They went out on the pitch divided. And yet, when the Flakelf side shouted their *"Heil Hitler!,"* the bakers spontaneously responded with a *"Fitzkult Hura!"* or "Long live sport!"—the motto of the Soviet teams.

Start played in red shirts, because there weren't any others for them. This chromatic happenstance ramped up the rivalry, emphasizing the rebelliousness of a side made up not just of Ukrainian bakers, but of communist ones at that.

The referee allowed the Germans to commit all the fouls they liked, as though the Geneva Convention were on the side of their unsporting conduct. They still went in 3–1 down at halftime.

In the break, an official went and spoke to the prisoners, leaving them in no doubt as to the consequences should they go on to win. This time the consensus was instantaneous: they would not let themselves be beaten. They won the match 5–3.

The details of what happened next were for many decades unclear. According to legend, the eleven players of Start were lined up and shot immediately afterward, the game coming to be known as "the match of death."

In fact, the Nazi revenge didn't take place immediately, but the punishment meted out altogether deserved the title. One of the more notoriously militant players was tortured, eventually dying from the treatment, and the others were all taken to Syrets concentration camp.

As prisoners, the Kiev bakers were given a 150-gram loaf of bread a day. On February 24, 1943, the head of the camp carried out some morbid equations, factoring the cold against the remaining rations. The snow was coming down, the inmates were starving, and there weren't sufficient calories available in the stores to keep everyone alive. By some delirious arithmetic, he decided to liquidate one in three of the inmates. Three members of the Start team died that same day.

When the Red Army took back Kiev in November, the population had fallen from four hundred thousand to eighty thousand. The relief of liberation was a relative thing for the players; in that panicked environment they were seen as collaborators who'd had the gall to play in a match with the enemy. The great daring they had shown in beating the Nazis held no weight. Nor did the fact the players had gone from being bakers under surveillance to inmates at a concentration camp. It was a time of reprisals and pillaging, and there was no room for nuance, let alone any assessment of the dwindling significance of a game of football.

The first report on the subject came out in 1959, when the health of the survivors was deteriorating and they'd begun to lose their memories.

But nothing is ever destroyed altogether, and the salient facts began to come to the surface.

A goal wasn't the biggest thing to happen in "the match of death." At one point the youngster Alexei Klimenko had shimmied through the defense and was in on goal, but—in one of the most important decisions in the history of the game—he chose not to slot the ball past the keeper, instead booting it back to the halfway line.

A deliberate miss—in the eyes of the Nazis, the worst thing of all. The Ukrainians, who had nothing at the time, allowed themselves to squander the goal and passed up on the chance to score.

And perhaps that was why Klimenko, the youngest member of the team, was one of the three selected in the "survival" round at the concentration camp. He was shot in the head.

Alexei Klimenko's achievement was an ethical non-shot. When he was in front of goal, in a position to finish off his captors, he chose instead to show that he was different from them: by letting them off.

THE FOOTBALL
AND THE HEAD

1. DIFFERENT PASSIONS

I imagine that at the end of a chess tournament, Karpov and Kasparov probably start seeing things: people's noses morphing into knights that let them know to check their eyes. Football fever is no different. You might find in these pages the occasional hint of good sense, but bear in mind that once, when I had an actual fever, I came to the conclusion that if cough medicines were football players, the most fearsome midfield would be a powerful composite of Robitussin, Breacol, and Zorritone. *In extremis*, the football fan has a very ball between the ears. He rarely defends what he thinks, being too nervous thinking about what it is that's being defended. When his team steps onto the pitch, the world, the ball, and the mind become one and the same thing. Utterly integrated into the scene, the fanatic turns to prayer or the stroking of rabbit feet.

It would be an exaggeration to say that the few people who don't partake of football hate it. In spite of the obvious deficiencies of those who believe it makes a difference to roar "*síquitibum!*" (fans of the Mexico national team), "*Visca el Barca*" (Barcelona FC), "*dale, dale Bo*" (Boca Juniors) or "*hala Madrid!*" (Real Madrid), there are still some who react to the sport with mere indifference.

But that isn't to say there aren't plenty of people who enjoy adding to the bonfire of the footballs. Hatred can be enjoyable, a pleasure you cultivate, and perhaps football serves the secret function of annoying those people who honestly just want to *be* annoyed. Every so often a Nostradamus with no apocalypse on the agenda turns up at a match, wets a finger, and decides the wind is blowing ill. How is it that multitudes succumb to such a petty vice? The diagnosis grows increasingly dire when the World Cup interrupts the usual TV schedule, not to mention weddings: friends who beforehand seemed in good mental health begin peppering the conversation with the unpronounceable names of Croatian left backs. To rail against bad taste is, however, pointless: our friend Maria will forever prefer her mangoes green, just as Nicole Kidman will always go for beaus who are impossible to like.

The blights that accompany the kicking of footballs are many. A quick inventory of the things that cannot be magicked away by the team doctor's medicine box: nationalism, violence in stadiums, commodification, and the objectionable sight of people with painted faces. All of this is obviously worthy of censure. But the pleasure we take in imagining things—there's no fighting that. Every fan finds his or her own made-to-measure pleasure—or perversion—on a football pitch. In a world where some find Cathar poetry erotic and for others it's edible underwear, it makes perfect sense that different people react differently. Ireland takes

waving the banner of certain clubs as a way of making up for their crimes and misdemeanors. Anyone wanting to find out about the dreadful deeds that football can give rise to need only spend a season with the Ultra Bad Boys, a group of Red Star Belgrade supporters. Franklin Foer did precisely this, and his book *How Soccer Explains the World: An Unlikely Theory of Globalization* provides transcriptions of the intellectual exchanges between the Red Start fanatics: "Who do you hate the most?" the interviewer asked one appropriately heavily tattooed individual. "Croats, cops, don't mind. I'd kill either." It's chilling to think someone "doesn't mind" in this regard, though such indifference doesn't extend to murder methods, the Ultra Bad Boys' weapon of choice being the metal bar.

What's so lamentable about Red Star, what makes it seem like a bad joke, is that though it's the police's favorite team a large number of its fans are involved in organized crime.

I traveled to Yugoslavia at the beginning of the 1980s and heard the same thing time and again, the same refrain about Tito being the country's rightful representative: "All the rest, they're just Serbs, Croats, Slovenes, Montenegrins..." But long before Marshal Tito's integrationist dreams exploded into a war, Serbo-Croat tensions were detonating in fights between fans of Red Star and Dinamo Zagreb.

A character emerged from the tatters of the post-Cold War country, one straight out of a John Le Carré novel: Željko Ražnatović. A secret-police hit man during the socialist era, he moved up a rung to gangster as capitalism dawned in the country. After bumping off several Muslims, his gusto for taking people's lives led him to start using the alias of "Arkan."

The son of an air-force pilot, Ražnatović dropped out of navy school and fled to Paris, where he became a small-time criminal. In Foer's summary of his incendiary CV: "In 1974, the Belgians locked him up for armed robbery. Three years later, he broke free from prison and fled to Holland. When the Dutch police caught him, he somehow managed to slither away from prison again... Back in Belgrade, he reconciled with his father and then worked his connections to the Yugoslav security apparatus." Like so many criminals, Arkan was a puritan, only evil. On a trip to Milan, we learn, a friend invited him to an orgy, but he passed, opting to stay in his room and do his keep-fit exercises instead.

A Red Star fanatic, he took on one of the strangest jobs in the world of football. The Serbian Communist Party secretary at the time, Slobodan Milošević, asked him to infiltrate the Ultras and start organizing them to suit the party's ends. Arkan brought discipline to the Red Star fanatics, and all the different factions ended up falling in behind him. His own Spartan conduct began to pervade the stands, and the stadium seemed to have been brought to heel. The only unchoreographed thing that happened there was the ravens flying up as a goal was celebrated.

But Milošević and Arkan had their minds on bigger prizes. Out of the Red Star Ultras an informal army was born: Arkan's Tigers. They even saw action, in the Serbian offensive of 1991–92. The violence, once spontaneous in the stands, became a matter of military tactics in a war—though perhaps "pillaging" is a better word for the actions of these cruel torturers. At the end of the genocide the scoreboard read: two thousand dead, and a fortune amassed in the looting.

Symbolically enough, Arkan moved into a house opposite Red Star's stadium. The locals viewed him as a pop idol, the hard guy who turned the hooligans into something "useful" at the same time as defending Serbia's honor.

Arkan wanted to use his war booty to buy the club he so loved, and when that wasn't possible he made do with another Belgrade side, FK Obilić. At least in name it seemed made to measure, Miloš Obilić having been a warrior who, the night before the Battle of Kosovo in 1389, slipped through enemy lines and assassinated Sultan Murad. The fortunes of Arkan's side quickly improved, due partly to referees worrying what would happen if they penalized a side backed by a group of paramilitaries.

The kinds of excesses you usually associate with managers and executives pale in comparison to Arkan's abuses of power, though this particular gangster's arc ended in the usual way when he was shot down in the vestibule of a hotel.

Arkan's strange legend folded in nationalist hopes, alternative centers of power, discipline in the eye of chaos, and sporting supremacy, and to this day the man still has his adherents in Belgrade, especially among the ever-expanding Ultra Bad Boys, whose numbers show no signs of abating. And his shift from criminality to the kind of illegal activities that went unpunished was all part of the country's convulsive recent past, a truly bloody episode but of the kind that became the norm for many Serbians, an anomaly not dissimilar to the presence of the ravens in Red Star's stadium.

ONE FOR ALL: FRANCESCO TOTTI

Let's halt this impure train of words for a moment to consider a unique case of love for a club. In the ever-shifting world of transfers and agents, there has been one gladiator who has refused to change course, however tempting the song of the sirens. He has plied his trade in Serie A, which is usually more than enough for great players, but for Roma, a side that spent long years in the wilderness before winning a *scudetto*, after the title machine Fabio Capello took over (leaving not long after, griping as usual).

The legend of Francesco Totti, immune to big money offers and the seduction of other shirts, has been a rare one in these globalized times. He was born in the Eternal City, but in one of its less hallowed spots. The writer Fernando Acitelli took it upon himself to count the steps between the Totti household and the imperial wall, and it turned out to be 264, just a few more than the length of a football pitch. The man beyond the wall went on to become the city's symbolic heart. Maybe it had to happen in Rome—there's almost too much symbolism there for it to have been otherwise. The fans have a flag that reads *Caput Mundi*: all roads lead to Rome, center of the world.

Totti is the only footballing superstar who has felt emotionally incapable of playing for another side. At the height of his fame, there were all kinds of sponsors clamoring to bathe in the reflected glory of his monomania. *Quo vadis?* The question simply didn't apply. And yet there was a moment when Totti was more future than present, and, like any legionnaire, he felt the conflicting pull. But he resisted. He would go on to be an arrogant and at times dirty player, but, as the narcissistic Roman tradition dictates, and with a sentimentalism some find distasteful, when he lost control he'd always look to make amends—and above all, he never left. Francesco Totti, a.k.a. the addiction to belonging. If the Tiber doesn't cross seven hills, the city's worth nothing.

The Roman forward went through the single sentimental excess that Maradona could not: sedentariness. Totti is the ultimate stay-at-homer. Other *calcio* divas have had faces perfect enough to stamp on coins, but only he has done enough to merit the insignia of the truly untransferable.

In the strangely ascetic world of Italian football, where pleasure, like the tiny dark drops in a *café ristretto*, is at a premium, forwards are solitary creatures, hard-running and lonely. There he is, Francesco Totti, chasing lost causes, showing that one person at least *is* the city. Roma may be defeated, but still he stays on.

ABSOLUTE LOONS

Football is loved by too many people not to be enjoyed in a thousand different ways. It's the most effective means ever invented for selling merchandise. No small thing when you compare it to other businesses. When all else fails, and the world seems to be on a constant downward spiral, TV will always come up trumps.

Money is what makes clubs go round, and in large measure it's also what decides results. Real Madrid spent seven hundred million euros in the same period of time that tiny Osasuna spent ten million. It seems inconceivable that they should both be in the same league. But then again Osasuna have a very good record against Real, especially when they were under the stewardship of Javier Aguirre, and there's also the fact that professional football has always been a stranger to economic justice.

Let us accept the inevitable: football represents other aspects of society in very complex ways, and it also allows for enormous stupidities. The beautiful game does awaken mankind's propensity to shout and scream, but the best argument against this criticism isn't rational, and it isn't through ideas about the purity of the game.

In its democratic approach to passion, football incorporates the widest range of defects. When all goes well, it means, inoffensively enough, that people act badly in the stands rather than at home. How many living-room heart attacks have been averted by people diverting their vociferous behavior to the stadium?

Football's like fiber in your diet: you don't want it to be all you have, but a certain amount is good for clearing you out. People bring a lot to football, and so a lot gets eliminated there. We can hardly judge it by the sublime protocols one associates with opera, given that its very reason is to vent emotional excesses, to let the lunatic inside each of us take control for ninety minutes so that the person who comes home from the match is, if no great humanist, at least reasonably normal.

Is there any way to classify the brief mental downgrade we undergo during a match? To be truly legitimate, a fan's defects shouldn't cause offense. So we come to the nub: if trying to resist football is pointless, proselytizing is also unlikely to get others on our side. No one can be convinced to "theoretically" delight in a goal. To talk about an enthusiasm that is so widely shared, as well as so vulgar, we need some other entry points.

Truly great moves have nothing to do with athletic capabilities, but a secret skill, in great part down to a psychological fine-tuning: Zidane filters a ball through a space containing exactly nothing, but into which Raúl is about to rush; Romário feints one way, left, and all eyes in the stadium follow; Valderrama stops, drops his arms to his side and goes to sleep standing up, like a siesta that is in fact the most surprising form of attack, the calm before the goal; Ronaldinho does all the above and still has time to thread it through to Eto'o.

There have been players—and Menotti is the best example—who didn't achieve fairytale feats but could run their mouths like nobody's business on the pitch. "So should I start running now?" El Flaco would ask an opponent, who then took his eye off the ball, not knowing that football was a tutorial on grass.

In trying to understand astonishing feats, the sports reporter ought to renounce all reason. Can anyone boast their way into a superior comprehension of the game? Of course not. The braggart won't even really convince himself. Every witness plays against his or her own shadow, in the style of Gesualdo Bufalino: "Every day I take penalties against myself. Fortunately, or unfortunately, I always hit the post." Football is wholly subjective: the spectator challenges his or her self and in trying to analyze everything in sight, once and for all and for everyone else, is bound to hit the post. In the never-ending activity of confusing the football and the head, there's no way out.

THE SENSE OF TRAGEDY

To exist, the singular maestro requires a certain drama to surround him. Though footballers' biographies are never as heartbreaking as those of ice skaters or Russian ballerinas, there needs to have been a certain amount of suffering in the past to generate the desire to shoot on goal. In 1998, during the World Cup in France, I attended one of Brazil's training sessions. There are few things as tedious as watching the herd or regiment trotting around, and truly talented players also find it tedious and look for ways out.

That afternoon, Giovanni and Rivaldo broke off during a pause and played a game of hit the crossbar. Giovanni managed it five times in a row, Rivaldo three. Never in my life have I witnessed a useless feat of such exactitude. No person is born with such guidance systems inbuilt. You need to either come from a broken or disadvantaged home, or just a very strange one, to achieve such levels of obsessive virtuosity. Giovanni and Rivaldo hoped to get something out of their diligent target practice that is impossible to explain.

Like trekking or ballet, football allows for the sublimation of suffering into physical discomfort. Those less skilled at converting trauma into touches on the ball end up playing in defense, and those whose problems outweigh their talent specialize in the football version of "acting out," by breaking up the game, or other players' ankles.

We know very well from Tolstoy that happy families don't generate novels. Nor do they produce footballers. You need to be very thirsty for consolation to want to put yourself on display in front of a hundred thousand baying fans and millions of prying media eyes. Opera singing, record breaking—it all points to something nasty in a person's history.

In team sports, the sense of tragedy needs to be shared by the collective. If we think about Holland, their football story lacks drama. Rembrandt's native country has enough chiaroscuro to fuel fights in bars, or even to make Harry Mulisch's novels interesting, but its players lack the necessary dose of agony to win matches. It's all the fault of the legendary Clockwork Orange: in the 1974 World Cup, Holland was such a goal machine that they could have put a gardener in goal and still won. Their captain Johan Cruyff wore the number 14—unheard of in those days, even slightly irreverent—and defied all the norms by popping up all over the pitch. It was at the World Cup in Argentina that they perfected their system of "total football," with players constantly swapping positions and rotating around the pitch, and it actually bordered on sadism with the inclusion of two identical twins, the van der Kerkhofs: their opponents were forever confusing René and Willy. In 1974 and 1978 Holland was ahead of its time and dominated everyone, but lost in both finals against less brilliant teams who nonetheless knew how to channel their inner pain to win trophies.

The '74 Holland side lost to Germany, a side of veterans who took more pride in their scars than in their skills (some of these warhorses had taken part in epic losses, including the 1966 Wembley final defeat and the semifinal in Mexico in 1970). The only person to criticize the Clockwork Orange's bullying approach with any eloquence was Anthony Burgess, who always saw football as little more than a vulgarity and at the time was concerned that his novel would come to be associated not only with a film he didn't much like, but with a group of eleven sweaty Dutchmen. All the other commentators saw Holland as heralding a renaissance on the pitch, and yet they lost to the long-suffering Germans, as four years later they would lose against the long-suffering Argentines (Menotti's side lacked stars and, strictly speaking, played against itself, in that they needed to shake off the support of their own military government as well as the disdain in which Argentine players traditionally held the national side).

Perhaps these great Holland sides were never crowned World Champions precisely because they had it all to lose, and a secret compensatory law exists whereby the champions must show up already in some way battered and bruised.

WHEN IT COMES DOWN TO IT, GERMANY WINS

The 1954 World Cup in Switzerland was meant to be the confirmation of the supremacy of the Hungary team of the day. Though in 1950 Brazil had lost on their home turf, and against all odds, no World Cup had ever had such clear favorites. Going into it, Hungary hadn't lost a match in four and a half years.

Their route to the World Cup had included wins over England, a 6–2 at Wembley and a 7–1 in Budapest. It went down in the memories of fans who would never see the Danube but learned on those days what Kocsis, Hidegkuti, and Bozsik had in their boots. The sun they orbited around was Ferenc Puskás, who was more than capable of scoring with that left foot of his from a hundred feet out. The '54 Hungary side can be considered the first to put 4-2-4 into practice and the first to really make full use of their central midfielders—that is, to understand that goals can be generated in the middle of the park, too. The goalkeeper Gyula Grosics was way ahead of his time, spraying pinpoint passes around from his penalty box. Apart from Hidegkuti, all the Hungarian stars played for the army team, Honvéd. They'd therefore been familiar with one another for a long time, and by mutual agreement played other sports together as well, to make themselves stronger and fitter. A veritable communist utopia on the pitch.

Unsurprisingly, the Hungarians notched up seventeen goals in their first two matches at Switzerland '54, the most significant being the 8-3 win over Germany, with Puskás out injured. When the two sides met again in the final, there couldn't have been anyone who expected anything but a win for Hungary.

What did Germany use to deny fate? The same quality they've always had on the pitch: the capacity to transform their suffering into epic feats. Their captain, Fritz Walter, was a thirty-three-year-old veteran with a fear of flying. He'd been a parachutist in the war and had watched his best friend die in front of him. He led a handful of younger but just as ruined players.

The trainer, Sepp Herberger, was one of those profoundly rational eccentrics that Germany produces every now and then. In the first match against Hungary he'd sent out a surprise team, as though, defeat being inevitable, he wanted to save his first eleven's energies. Everything he said, though, contradicted that idea, which, when it came down to it, was actually a kind of praise. Each time he was asked about the fate of a certain match, he would answer in the same way: "The ball is round." As though it was all down to chance, or the will of God, once the whistle blew.

Puskás was carrying an injury, and there was a lot of speculation about the unlikelihood of him appearing in the final. The Germans, in a move many interpreted as advance capitulation, offered to lend the Hungarians their doctors—which the Hungarians haughtily refused.

Herberger's great spark came on the eve of the final. In that hoarse, slow voice of his, the German trainer explained that in normal conditions the Magyars would be superior, but that if it rained things might be different. As Victor Hugo said of Napoleon, Waterloo was lost because the rain prevented him from using his artillery so well and stymied his painstaking cavalry charges. Bad weather favors those who can adapt to mud and disorder. And when Herberger felt the first drop of rain, he knew the final in Bern was going to be an episode of trench warfare, a chance for the courageous to win the day.

Let's cast our minds back to the most famous about-turn in history. No final had ever bucked expectations like this one was about to. Hungary scored two goals in eight minutes—unsurprisingly. Fritz Walter got his team together and said some words that no one else heard and that were never known to anyone besides them. What could this man—who only had to hear a jet engine to fall to pieces—have possibly communicated? What was contained in his agonizing dispatches?

The film *The Miracle of Bern* describes the numerous expectations unleashed by the match: for some it was verification of the German disaster after the Nazi delirium, and for others a recuperation of the nation's joy. It had begun badly, but everything was about to change. It was also around this time that the England striker Gary Lineker was born, and as he would later go on to say, "Football is a simple game. Twenty-two men chase a ball for ninety minutes, and at the end, the Germans always win."

Had they played ten more times, Hungary might have won nine times against the Germans. But it was raining that day, and Germany knew how to make the most of a difficult situation. The final ended 3-2, with the tragic kings of the spherical lifting the cup.

Let's pause a moment and consider a concept that takes in a history of national mentalities and perhaps even the transmigration of souls: tradition. Some teams always lose in certain stadiums for the simple reason that they have always lost there. Little matter if they show up undefeated and with a guy leading the line wearing golden Nike boots. The rigid determinism of footballing traditions can be quite overwhelming. All the players who lost on the previous occasion might have moved to other sides or retired, but the new representatives of the team are wearing the same shirt; tradition is going to step in and, without fail, snatch the ball from them at decisive moments.

Such myths do sometimes come tumbling down, but football's ghosts aren't overcome lightly. Something along these lines happened in 1974 and 1978. In the Germany World Cup, Holland played wonderful football but lacked the tradition a team acquires by swallowing bitter pills. West Germany's play was encumbered, predictable; they lost against East Germany, just about beat Chile, and felt under huge pressure from their fans, who were desperately casting around for reasons to feel pan-Germanic. Success seemed unlikely. But they were supported by the many long shadows of those who had suffered in the name of the team. Their captain was Franz Beckenbauer, the young *libero* who had dazzled in the 1966 World Cup in England. Never has a player had better posture than Beckenbauer or been able to run so menacingly without the ball at his feet. When Heidegger, who knew nothing about the sport, went to a match, he was astonished by the determination shown by a young player, one whom destiny would later smile upon: it was of course none other than the player who came to be known as "Der Kaiser."

In the two previous World Cups, the captain of Germany had had his fair share of heartache. In 1966 he saw the trophy stolen by a phantom goal (the Soviet linesman who gave the goal later confessed that body language affected his decision: the German goalkeeper looking crestfallen, the English striker wheeling away with his arms in the air; the symbolism signifying "goal" was so familiar to him he accepted it as a substitute). In Mexico '70 he'd been on the losing side in the "game of the century" against Italy—he'd played with a dislocated shoulder, held in place by a bandage from the Great War.

In contrast, Holland were a happy bunch. They drank wine, smoked a cigarette or two at halftime, and were allowed visits from their girlfriends or wives (sometimes their girlfriends *and* wives). The Germans arrived in the final as though they'd been transported to the Russian Front. And won, naturally.

And what about the '78 Argentina side? In front of their own fans, they lost against Italy, and then stuffed Peru with what seemed suspicious ease. But they were representing the country of Di Stéfano, Sívori, Pedernera, and other geniuses who never won World Cups but should have. Menotti's men were carried along by debts accumulated over various generations.

There's no way to calibrate the historical suffering that unbalances two matches. If a defender suspects his wife of having cheated on him with a friend while he was staying at the team hotel, the suffering is real but not of historical proportions. The following day he's going to score the most superb goal. Whereas the pain of those previously in the same situation becomes even stronger, because it's a compound of a long history. The great revelation in the film about King Pelé is to do with the moment when he, as a boy, listened to the 1950 final on the radio, bearing witness to Brazil's defeat at the Maracanã. It was out of this fissure that his will to win the trophy three times was born—it was the same trophy he'd felt the loss of as a child.

But then, how difficult to make Holland even care! In the 2000 European Championships, they were the continent's best-shaved team. They were on home soil, so the stands filled with their joyous trumpeters. Patrick Kluivert missed two penalties in a single match, and the cameras showed only a blissful smile on his face, like he was attending a country fair. Proof of how minor the repercussions are of being poleaxed in the Low Countries.

But let's not make this an encomium to disaster only; it's just to point out that in Brazil the equivalent would have sent the priests out to decapitate chickens by the thousand and disabled people to throw themselves into the sea in their wheelchairs. The only time Holland will win the World Cup is when they are a less happy country and allow themselves to feel the effect of complexes and frustrations from which, to date, they have been blithely disconnected.

BEAUTIFUL DEFEAT

A sense of the tragic can be remarkably helpful, and yet football also sometimes resembles a *ranchera*, the ubiquitous melodramatic Mexican folk song, and the best thing to do can be to simply feel outraged, singing, "How could we lose like that?!"

The Frenchman Christian Karembeu, who played a costly second-string artist at Real Madrid, would magnetize all the camera flashes as the team left the pitch; something in his face matched the epic anguish perfectly, the sense of a leader dethroned. Karembeu was one of those giants of the game who seemed subject to the judgments of destiny rather than the paying public. Obviously his capacity for looking so damned, but at the same time so damned good, was of more use to photographers and journalists than it was to the club.

Others capitalize on tragedy even more effectively. The Portuguese goalkeeper Vítor Baía was an elegant cultivator of his own indifference. Like those happy Dutchmen, the ex-Barcelona keeper poured most of his energy into sculpting his facial hair: his sideburns could have been Dalí's handiwork. Perhaps it was because he hailed from the country of *saudade* that his melancholy manner was able to reach such splendorous heights each time he conceded a goal. Not much help in winning matches, but his chic outward shows of distress did at least ensure the reputation of this sublime martyr.

Baía's crepuscular abilities can perhaps be extended to his country, too. Every time the World Cup comes around, Mexican commentators go crazy for the Portuguese side, one of the reasons being that we would love to be able to lose like them. They manage to play amazing football for a couple of matches, and they even produce goal-scoring defenders. And they're good-looking in an interesting way. They have the mien of those for whom things have not gone well but who are ready (with our support) for a swift turnaround. Unfortunately though, come game three, without fail they're hurling abuse at the ref. It's hard to find a national team that feels so little responsibility for their defects. Reporters, drawn in by the charisma of the Portuguese, go along with them for longer than you'd usually expect and try to find very strange ways to explain away their tendency for such elegant collapses. The Lusitanian rejection of success reached its zenith in the 2004 European Championships, which were held in Portugal. One local journalist summed it up perfectly: "Our players are completely lacking in vice: they don't smoke, they don't drink, and they don't perform either."

So great is the Portuguese players' dedication to art for art's sake that their faulty touches in 2004 could be seen as a paradoxical kind of efficiency. No one expected them to reach the final, where they met a Greece side that had been transformed by the disciplinarian Otto Rehhagel into awkwardness itself. Football was on Portugal's side, but so was their propensity for sorrow. And, true to themselves, they let the trophy slip through their hands. We Mexicans became admirers once more, knowing we'd never lose with such style.

Colombia has also done their bit for the psychology of defeat. Francisco Maturana's side beat Argentina 5-0 on the eve of the 1994 World Cup and looked sure to go on to greater things. For the previous four years they had been a well-choreographed threat, with the shaggiest hairdos and the sparsest beards, an imbalance in the hair department worthy of musketeers or pirates. They also had a number of black players who would seem to be wandering around asleep, before suddenly sprinting a hundred yards in record time. The team's guiding lights, Higuita and Valderrama, belonged to that class of Latin Americans who need a little injection of angst before they can show they actually care. Both were so utterly self-assured that when a match kicked off it was as though they'd just finished one. It took such effort for them to even get on the field of play that there was no way they were then going to submit to everyone else's rules; they attempted perilous and pointless moves simply to demonstrate how abysmal the necessary ones are. Never has a goalkeeper transmitted such self-satisfaction as Higuita as he rushed from his area to clear the ball, as though he were in some barrio alleyway, or when he did one of his famous scorpion kicks, clearing the ball off the line in the most audacious way.

For his part, Valderrama embodied a phrase given to me by the poet Darío Jaramillo Agudelo: "We play wonderful football, only in slow motion." To have a midfielder who was never in a hurry wasn't entirely opportune, considering this is a sport where his opponents did run. His equanimity was a question of principle, and his calm was superlative when all about him were losing their heads. Valderrama would have been able to get annoyed with the firing squad when they raised their rifles; the sentence would have been annulled.

Colombia played in 1990 and 1994 as though they had a license to lose. Which made them different from the great Peru side of Mexico '70 under Didi, who also played with a fearless optimism but gave everything to win until the final whistle. The Colombians operated with a kind of consummate playfulness. They ruled the scoreboard, even if the result went against them. No one ever beat them; they orchestrated their own downfalls. In contrast to meritocracy and the vulgar customs of winning, the great Colombia side of those four years showed that the outcome was a highly subjective matter. Masters when it came to straying from the accepted path, they would never debase themselves by worrying about success. Higuita would take a free kick and have to dash back to his goal faster than his legs could carry him. And yet the danger of a counterattack was always pleasing to him.

The Colombian prodigies never wanted any other prize to come their way. Has there ever been a more Latin American feat than that of these buccaneers, masters of rebellious dignity, when they put on a show and didn't worry about the prize?

So Colombia was the greatest proponent of a tendency we admire, without ourselves ever having mastered it. The Mexican national team's war cry translates as "Yes, we can!" Since we expect defeat, it isn't enough to tell our players we love them and that they're great; it's imperative we make sure they understand that there is actually a chance they might win something.

PRETEND PASSION

There's such a range of behaviors on display at a football pitch, there's no way of codifying them, above all because many are so hypocritical. An arena where pure ego dresses up as humility and consummate skill is employed to cheat refs, this game is dependent on acts of simulation, some as naturalistic as that of the Chile keeper Roberto "Cóndor" Rojas in September 1989. The stage was the Maracanã, the opponent Brazil, and the aim to qualify for Italia '90. The Chilean number 1 went onto the pitch with a razor blade hidden inside one of his gloves. Seeing the unlikelihood of Chile coming back after Careca put Brazil ahead, he waited for a firework to pass close to his goal and, when nobody was looking, sliced his own forehead with the blade. When the referee came over, Rojas claimed the firework had hit him. Though the scoreline would remain the same even if the game were abandoned, if they could prove that the game shouldn't have been played under the circumstances, they'd be able to go to the negotiating table. The strangest thing about the tale is that Rojas ended up confessing. FIFA suspended him from professional football permanently.

I met a man a few years ago who had died two hundred times. He worked as a body double in *narco* movies and in the occasional Western filmed in Durango. He was an expert in falling down stairs and off balconies and in being run over. He retired with a bad back, and the painkillers he took gave him an ulcer—a pretty decent trade-off in his line of work.

He was a specialist in dying photogenically, which would have made him very well suited to being a footballer. In no other sport do you come across such extreme levels of histrionics. Suddenly a striker is flying through the air, coming to ground after a spectacular pirouette, flailing on the grass, hands to face, convulsing, all in the hope of a red card for the tackler, or at the very least a yellow.

What next for the athlete of the death rattle? On come the medics with the sponge, the bottles of water, and in a matter of seconds he'll have recovered, the damage no greater than some wet hair and an untucked shirt. Like an amphitheater of resurrection, football offers the spectacle of the dead not only returning, but running. And it's easy to tell when someone really has been hurt, because they lie there doing nothing.

Simulation is common practice. Referees can watch matches on TV as well, so they know who the divers are and sometimes don't even award them free kicks when they are actually fouled. And when that happens, the censure the player receives, the whistles, howls, and boos, seem to contain the pride of unmasking not just one, but a hundred boys that cried wolf.

You could never imagine the batter in a baseball game throwing himself to the floor and pretending that the pitcher had thrown an invisible ball; in American football, you'd never get a quarterback halting his run to make out that someone had treated him "too rough." Only in football do we find these fabricated fouls. This is partly because the refs and linesmen make more mistakes. If a player is sharp and particularly mischievous, he can get one over on the man in black whose grueling task it is to keep within viewing distance of the action.

There was a contretemps in France '98 that summed up perfectly the power of pantomime. Diego Simeone, the Argentine who had been the very symbol of fortitude in his club careers with Atlético Madrid and Inter Milan, demonstrated his love of the limelight in the match against England. The encounter between the two nations had been so hyped you'd have thought the fate of the Falklands hung on it. The first half exceeded all expectations with an epic, hard-fought 2–2, including a goal from Michael Owen on his national debut. But in the second half David Beckham had a run in with "Cholo" Simeone; sprawled on the floor, Beckham kicked out, discreetly but clearly intentionally. Up until this point, the affair had been governed by the quarrelsome logic of the animal kingdom, but then came Simeone's Elizabethan revenge: Cholo collapsed on the floor like a skewered Mercutio, a display that turned what should have been a yellow into red. A couple of years later, Beckham's Manchester United met Simeone's Inter, and the Argentine held up his hands to the deceit. If a hardworking battler like Simeone sometimes plays the comedian, it's fairly obvious what's going to happen with players whose *only* recourse is to theatrics. Like the film double with his two hundred deaths, certain footballers make a living from dying, but not really.

THE NEED FOR SPEED

As the name suggests, Nandrolone is an untrustworthy drug, one that makes you run faster but can also cause liver cancer. No one takes it for the nice taste. But sometimes representing your country means traveling from Australia to Korea, and from there to Texas, and somewhere along the way someone giving you a chicken that's been pumped full of hormones. And if you end up being chosen to urinate in a bottle after a match, suddenly your career is in danger.

There has, it's true, also been the odd case of athletes drugged not by unluckily consuming some triple-continental chicken breasts, but by the physical trainer! Pep Guardiola, at the time Barcelona's model captain, was on the wrong end of a dope ruling in Italy. The impression the fans had, in this case, was that something had gone wrong on the game's pharmaceutical front and that the problem must have been the doctor, or doctored lab results.

Some therapists are convinced that the player needs support on two levels: the muscular and the spiritual. The second is obviously more slippery. It isn't easy consoling a homesick player, or one who doesn't know why he's sick and whom you find staring at tables as though they were the league tables and he's about to get relegated. Here's where motivational patches come in. Footballers breakfast on the kind of pills you'd expect at an astronaut's banquet. Not all of them are vitamins; some are antioxidants, and others help bring down swelling—the last kind decides whether the doctor keeps his job. When they claim that doping doesn't help you to play like Maradona, it only means that the stimulants in their prescriptions are harder to detect.

Multimillion-dollar businesses hang on the fortunes of modern football teams, twice a week. This has made for severe tensions between the use of chemical remedies and their possible discovery. Energy boosters are the superstitious laboratory expedient in an activity that requires Rivaldo to be able to run very fast on Sunday, though he has been walking for the last year as though he just stepped on a cactus. For elite sides, these tonics are like life after death; it's worth believing in them, just on the off-chance they happen to be efficacious.

No team is free of pills or physiological paranoia. To fend off a world that can force them to urinate at random any given Sunday, squads get together in five-star prisons where they eat closely guarded veal cutlets. And there, the boredom they endure has the same effect on the soul as doping does on the heart.

PASSION INHIBITORS

The fear of sexual contact is just as great as the fear of rogue pharmaceuticals. It's not unheard of for coaches to send out flotillas of prostitutes against the enemy hotel. Before unleashing his forces, he gives them the team talk: the idea is not to satisfy the opposition, but to submit them to a grueling, porn-film kind of discomfort, reducing them to scraps of men.

Such exhaustion can be avoided if you allow conjugal visits. But when it comes to football, everything is almost entirely metaphysical. Though you get some permissive clubs (almost all of the Dutch and the Scandinavian sides), many of the physical trainers prioritize a certain conventional wisdom, secure in the certainty that any player who ejaculates the night before a match loses the desire for the transcendent orgasm substitute that is the goal. The erotic is just as much part of dietary control as boiled vegetables.

Enduring all of this is nothing compared to the regular torture players have to endure, all the hours of doing nothing, nothing, and more nothing. When a team goes away together, what they have in common is the shirt, and the time wasting. When Ronaldinho plays his beloved Nintendo he likes to pick... Ronaldinho! Unfortunately not everyone can revel in such self-referential delights. Some get by playing cards or staring at the ceiling. These prolonged hotel nirvanas have the capacity to erode the brain imperceptibly, to the point that players might actually end up botching the job come match day, or say yes to appearing in advertisements for talcum powder.

The solitude of team get-togethers is extreme, because it is, among other things, a shared solitude. Your children turn into the photos printed on the T-shirt you sleep in; in contrast, your roommate is a smell too near. Even clubs who provide their players with Armani suits force players to double up in rooms. The rigors of personal branding are nothing compared to this forced cohabitation. I once asked a professional football player what he and his roommate talked about. The answer gave a glimpse into the rich world that is psychopathology: "He doesn't talk to me," the player said. "He talks to his penis. He calls it Ramón, and they talk about everything they've been through together." I wasn't surprised when, a short while afterward, the player in question— a courteous and calm individual who humbly used the word "penis" when talking to a journalist—was warming the bench. His roommate's monologues to Ramón had had their effect, and he started seeing things on the pitch that weren't there.

A football player has to combine the narcissism of someone who wants to be seen at all costs, the vocation of a monk to be shut away in a monastery, and the ability to put up with the stench of the fellow inmate. Has any person ever been born with such a combination in their nature?

While the stars wander zombie-like along the hotel passageways, there we are, the fans, speculating about what they'll do on the pitch. Their isolation opens a gap for prophecies to fill. Words either rush into football's "empty" hours, or prove that players are of such stuff as boredom is made on. We talk about what we cannot see. And then when we have the match there in front of us, we begin to talk about what we do not understand.

THE APPEARANCE OF THE INVISIBLE

A football pitch comes with whole basements full of superstitions, complexes, phobias, dramas, and dreams. What else but the most indeterminate and obscure reasons could explain the goal drought suffered by Fernando Morientes, the nullification of a player whose only quality was his efficiency in front of goal? And why, when he finally did score again and Roberto Carlos tried to celebrate with him, did he push him away? It was as though outrage was all he deserved, or as though he had only become himself again so that he could take revenge on his own team, not on the opposition. Did that gesture mean that even scoring couldn't make him feel right at Real Madrid? Had he spent so much time on the bench and playing out of position that his emotions themselves had been dislodged? Were his thoughts drifting toward another club already, one where he could play without the obligation of being a genius?

They wouldn't be mysteries if they proffered up their own answers. We can know that Morientes left Real for Monaco, but we'll never be privy to the agonizing that went into the decision, because, among other things, the player himself can't understand the tangle of emotions that prompt him to pack his bags. The exterior in football is so pleasing, so flashy, that the private life of goals gets obscured. And yet there are inner causes.

The strip between the pitch and the tunnel down to the changing rooms is called the "mixed zone." It's the closest the press can get to the facts. When the time comes to make a psychological evaluation of the game, there's no mixed zone for all realities and desires. The mind is also in play, but we're almost always unsure of its precise function. Such lack of definition only adds to the interest in a sport in which the great moves have their beginnings long before they become visible.

Football's attractiveness lies in its constantly renewing capacity to make itself incomprehensible. Something occurs, but we don't understand it—like grass growing, or our blood pumping around and around. Zidane suddenly happens upon a gap and plays the ball into it. What moves him? What idea, as yet uncertain, crystallizes in this forward movement? Without knowing the way it's going to go or how it's going to end, we feel the vibration of what might happen and, though not yet here, it is already of consequence. Zidane moves forward. The invisible is the one thing we can be sure of.

2. MENTALITIES

JUAN JOSÉ ARREOLA, PING-PONG HERALD

I once tried to get onto the Mexican Ping-Pong squad. This was in June 1970, two years before the Olympics came to Mexico, and even minor sports had suddenly taken on a mythical glow. I was fourteen at the time and had developed an interest in the games played in the kitchen-dining room of the writer Juan José Arreola; he'd installed a Ping-Pong table with a Chinese-lacquer top to ensure the perfect bounce.

Arreola was forever moving house but always stayed on the outskirts of Colonia Irrigación. ("I'll change rivers," he'd say, "but not to Mesopotamia.") At the time he was living on a street named Río Nilo (River Nile) and had developed an interest in the building of the Aswan Prison, on the other Nile, as though those dikes had something to do with the traffic coming along his street. I was quite defensive as a player, and he encouraged me to try a contentious shot that involved slicing down across the ball: "the Aswan Low Dam," he called it.

Every Saturday Arreola's apartment was divided between those of us who leaped around after the Ping-Pong ball, and the sedentary ones who played chess at the back, clouds of smoke billowing around them. There was barely any furniture in the place, which resembled a cross between a barrio social club and a salon for intellectuals. When the Maestro got hungry, he went into the kitchen and opened a bag of crisps. This meager fare he accompanied with careful sips from a silver hip flask that he kept in his jacket and never once allowed me to taste.

During our sporting marathons, the author of *Confabulario* would go from room to room reciting poems and sporting facts, eyes bulging, his gray curly hair a tousled mess.

Arreola had retired from his work as a mime artist, actor, artisan, cloth seller, and prose writer of Borgesian refinement, and his approach to sport was as an extension of words. He was more a herald than a reporter—a fanciful town crier. He spelled out *what might happen* in the matches, not deigning to describe the precariously real shots themselves. Extremely thin and extremely sprightly, he could get the heel of his foot up over his head, fakir-like. There was a theatrical liveliness in the way he walked, and he often went around in a frock coat that he claimed had belonged to José María Pino Suárez. He always moved somehow rapidly, putting me in mind of the Yamaha he kept on the lower floor and drove to the university. All of this was long before television would devour the immense orality of the long-winded mass of Mexican writers. These Saturdays of ours, Arreola would foretell the outcomes on the Ping-Pong table and the chessboards, using the suggestive phraseology of the fortune-teller to prophesy the outcomes.

Though his technical understanding was very good, his advice always tended toward the metaphorical. When I took part in a citywide table-tennis tournament, I was drawn against a formidable opponent in the first round, a player who could hit the ball in a way altogether contradictory to his first name: Modesto. He worked as a Metro driver, and similarly in Ping-Pong he evinced the kind of sureness that made it seem he was on rails. I was a newcomer, and my only strong point was my determination not to give up. When I told Arreola I was playing Modesto the thunderer, he pronounced these words: "Get him inside your chicken coop, and he won't be a peacock anymore!"

I lost badly, but never forgot the phrase. All sports owe something to the words that go around inside the players' heads. Certain expressions have the capacity to activate the mitochondria, prevent tiredness and sweating, keep you motivated in spite of adversity, and drive you on to win a trophy, that mysterious object that as an object is never much to look at but that everyone still wants to get their hands on. Arreola's pessimistic cries were more literature than stratagem, but they showed the intimate connectedness of physical exertion and the imagination.

Can the interior life of a sportsperson ever be fully calculated? The first response to a metaphysical question like this is that different sports mean different thoughts. I put Ping-Pong forward here as a contrast to football.

The games played in Arreola's apartment were meant to pass the time. Things were completely different when I went to the Mexican Olympic Center to ask to join the table-tennis team. I met Nobuyuki Kamata, a coach who had recently arrived from Japan, whose ideas about the sport were inflected by Zen philosophy. For Kamata, the sportsperson who knows how to concentrate can suppress the interior monologue and thereby pull off shots with a kind of automation that is alien to the nervous system. "He who thinks, loses," was Kamata's motto. Like the archer who unlooses the perfect arrow without being able to see the target, the Ping-Pong player, emptying the mind, ought to allow his hand to decide. To blank out the interior world like this requires monk-like discipline—something I was incapable of, whereas my sister Carmen mastered it, going on to become a national champion and even traveling to China. There she got to play some true experts in the art of operating at the margins of thought.

Ping-Pong is nonstop, a reflexive parenthesis, which is the reason why thoughts need to be dispensed with. In such rapid-fire territory, everything depends on instinct and reflexes. He who thinks, loses.

Strangely, Arreola's view was that football was a less intellectual sport than tennis or Ping-Pong, due to the lack of the intermediary racket. Its actions are grosser, in that they do not pass through a civilized instrument, and furthermore bypass the hands, a fundament of human culture. Tennis presupposes more complex historical developments; the scoring system is complex, and the rackets are testament to the kind of industry and ingenuity that get the best out of catgut.

Arreola was an admirer of sports that filtered through technology and craftsmanship. He was captivated by the supersensitive oilcloths used on the Swiss paddles in Ping-Pong, by the East/West division of the sport depending on how a player held the bat, and by the unassailable superiority of the Chinese lacquer. Though he was born in Jalisco, the cradle of Mexican footballing culture, the beautiful game struck him as regressive, a backward step to the days of mankind before tools.

Faced with Arreola's eloquence, there was nothing I could do to argue football's case. But in the same way that we true fanatics carry on arguing even once our interlocutor has gone away, I'll give the answer I was unable to give at the time. Football offers one of the most propitious situations for the intellectual life, in that the majority of the game is spent doing nothing. You run but the ball is nowhere near you, you stop, you do up your bootlaces, you shout things no one hears, you spit on the ground, you exchange a harsh look with an opposing player, you remember you forgot to lock the terrace door. For the majority of the game, the football player is no more than *the possibility of a footballer*. He or she can be in the game without being *in* the game. He or she has to be there for the group sketch to be complete, and has to move around to avoid being caught offside, or to shake off a marker. But there are long stretches in this strange state, being-nowhere-near-the-ball, since it's only in the zone immediately around the ball that the game truly takes place.

What this means is that the player spends their time thinking about what he or she should be doing on the pitch, or about utterly unrelated subjects that nonetheless affect performance. The goalkeeper, the great loner in the contest, has more time than anyone to reflect, which is why thinkers and eccentrics tend to gravitate to the position: the leaders and the clowns. All keepers know the rich interior life their profession entails. Constantly on guard, long periods pass with nothing to do, and yet, at any second, they might be called upon to make a save.

It could be that, to Arreola, an interior life of this kind seemed too bucolic, but this is the nature of the symposia that take place on turf.

MILOŠEVIĆ, SLOW SPRINTER

One of the most astonishing performances I have ever witnessed came from Savo Milošević in a 2005 match between Real Madrid and Javier Aguirre's Osasuna. Milošević was playing for Osasuna, and they were away from home. Osasuna went a man down, and then Valdo had to be stretchered off after a brutal tackle from Roberto Carlos. The *rojiblancos* had arrived at the Bernebéu on a high, second in the league, but everyone knew that the Basque club, run on a shoestring, would go to pieces come winter, like the horses of old that failed to make it to the racing track. What chance did their ten men have against star-studded Madrid? Milošević played in unusually inspired fashion, trying to get his teammates to simply play keep-the-ball. For most of the game he passed forward at the same time as sideways—sounds contradictory, but far from it; the veteran moved like an old, whipped nag, but carried on with his chess-knight-like moves. He held on to the ball, infuriating the opposition, then suddenly found a hole in behind. The Bernebéu got to its feet to applaud him when he scored a header—by no means his specialty. He'd single-handedly unhinged Madrid, so in a sense it wasn't a surprise that he should decide the contest. In a match dominated by Milošević and his sangfroid, his ability to put the ball to sleep, Madrid equalized through sheer weight of numbers. You'll never find it taught in any manual, because it's a trick that can't be programmed. Basically, all manuals *ought* to begin with the following phrase: "Football is too strange to predict."

Milošević put into action the paradox of Achilles and the tortoise. Extremely slow, sure of his movements, there was no way he was going to be caught by speedy Roberto Carlos. That night made me remember Arreola's words: "Get him inside your chicken coop, and he won't be a peacock anymore!"

ENOUGH, FOOLS!

Jorge Valdano recovered one of football's essential anecdotes. In 1969, the Argentine side Chacarita Juniors won the league against all expectations. A humble side, when they came out of nowhere to top the league they were coached by a man who spoke as resoundingly as his name suggested: Geronazzo. When they asked him how he did it, he said, "The first time I saw them play, I said to myself, 'No team can win if more than 30 percent of them are simpletons.' I lowered that percentage, and we won the league."

Foolishness, in football, may not be abused. Every team, as representative of the human condition, has to include a couple of dummies. It isn't that every midfielder needs a mind like Jules Verne, but he does need to move the ball in accordance not with what *is* happening, but according to what *might happen*. What distinguishes illustrious players from the athlete forcing himself to compete is that their prodigious acts only become possibilities in the moment when they occur; a second earlier, they were impossibilities.

The beautiful game involves skipping around, tugging shirts, and so on; it is a mechanical activity. But the decisive factor is the ghostly feint, the pass that makes a coconspirator of a gap, the ability to distress and send your opponents the wrong way, winning the ball back after you've seen what an opponent has in mind, anticipating hidden intentions.

Can a football player have such potency? Truly, this is no game for buffaloes. If a person spends the best part of their youth lounging in a hammock, it's highly unlikely they're going to be turning out in the shirt of top-flight sides in later life. But genius on a football pitch is another thing, determined by an attribute just as singular as paranoia, melancholia, or a sense of humor.

As Woody Allen tells it, Abraham Lincoln was very pleased when, one day, he was asked, "How long should a man's legs be?" It gave him the chance to deploy the obvious little apothegm "Long enough to reach the floor." It is with the same irrefutable common sense that we can state that a player is in good physical condition if his merits outweigh his tiredness. That is all.

You don't learn to be a trickster in the gym. The contract between man and ball is psychological, and surpasses mere physical effort. You can't have an amazing shot without two interior attributes taking pleasure in shooting and wanting to get better at it. This is the only way to explain the maniacal obsession of those who teach their feet, as it were, to speak many languages. How different a pile driver is from a volley off the instep or a shot off the outside of the foot!

Clearly, not all kinds of intelligence are useful in football. A strong capacity for abstract thought is in fact calamitous with a ball at your feet. What football demands is a mind so quick and self-assured that it meshes with physical reflexes, though it isn't precisely the same thing, as it presupposes a sequence, a next action, something still to come, when the move will make better sense. Romário, with three defenders surrounding him, in the blink of an eye would discover a way through them. He was one of the very few with the ability to drop a shoulder so confoundingly, showing the balance of a tightrope walker as he left the opposition in his wake and the nerves of a war correspondent as he put up with the attentions of his man-markers, and, ultimately, making the impossible space possible.

HOW TO BE HAPPY

Almost always, a goal is followed by a group hug and everyone trotting back to the halfway line. Sometimes the celebration gets skipped, say, if the team is losing 5–0 and the goal is a consolation—"consolation goal" anyway being a misnomer, because it only shows how much better the losing side could have played. Sometimes the celebration is a solo performance of jubilation—Paolo Rossi sliding along on his knees, Hugo Sánchez's somersaults, the outstretched arms of Careca wheeling away like a crop duster, Bebeto's imaginary baby in the cradle, Cardozo with his boot to his ear, like Super Agent 86's phone. In *Nuevas cosas del fútbol* (Football's New Things), the Chilean reporter Francisco Mouat creates an unforgettable typology of goals, with forty-six examples of celebrations—all these different ways of transmitting on-pitch delight to the fans—to match.

The people in the stands have found themselves perplexed by the ever-wilder post-goal displays, and how they come increasingly to occupy center stage. The celebrations of players with carnival tendencies can become more involved than the goal itself. With a dynamism he has never showed inside the game, a poacher who has just bundled the ball past the keeper from a few yards out might run all the way over to the cage keeping the ruggedest fans off the pitch and leap up onto the bars, whereas Hristo Stoichkov tore apart the widest array of defenses without showing the slightest emotion—aside from the intense grimaces that communicated his dislike for his rivals and, even more, for his teammates.

Mouat's typology includes "the dog"—a celebration once carried out by Cuauhtémoc Blanco. It was so filthy that it won him a booking, and it became one of those things you can't help but remember, little as you wish to. Blanco and a certain goalkeeper named Félix Fernández had been longstanding enemies. The contrasts between the pair were obvious, Blanco being a sewer rat, advancing along the pitch like he was keeping an eye out for a car mirror to steal, his shoulders hunched, his gait duck-like. He always had a mean look about him and would have tantrums that infuriated referees as much as they softened the hearts of *telenovela* actresses. He was *the* Mexican player between 1995 and 2005. Félix Fernández, on the other hand, willowy, always wearing those white gloves, is Mexican football's cultured man: a great columnist, involved in social work, a philanthropist who also liked to have a good time. Blanco perhaps felt him to be his enemy because the keeper was the paradigm of all the virtues favored by his parents, teachers, coaches, as well as the refs and linesmen who constantly berated him. Then one day fate pitted them against one another in the most direct way: a penalty. Cuauhtémoc was up front for América, Félix was in goal for Atlético Celaya, and it was the forward's chance to settle the score. Cuauhtémoc slotted it home, and then ran over to the line, got down on all fours, cocked a leg, and, doggy-style, pretended to mark his territory.

A constant in great goals is the keeper beautifying them by diving uselessly to try and save it. In this case, Félix faced Cuauhtémoc with aplomb and, rather than reacting, merely turned his thoughts to his next article.

Cuauhtémoc's celebration, like that of Hugo Sánchez when he

grabbed his testicles, belongs to the scatological kind of pride, and it isn't difficult to see why it gets punished. But there are other expressions of happiness that disconcert referees, and sometimes even FIFA itself.

Forwards of a romantic nature never miss the chance to seal their goals with a kiss. This can please family members or nations in need of some supportive therapy. At France '98, Rivaldo rained down kisses on his wife, and Zidane, Algerian by descent, kissed the blue shirt each time he scored—the most significant gesture of racial integration in the country in the postwar period, according to *Le Nouvel Observateur*.

Imagination, so often a deciding factor in moves on the pitch, also determines celebrations, and over-celebrations. There was a period when it became fashionable for the goal scorer to remove his shirt, baring underclothes with photos of the kids, a Madonna, or a "Save the Dolphins" message. This editorial variant on the celebration is the least spontaneous, as well as a good demonstration of why players are so rarely any good as journalists. As a way of stopping time wasting and controversy, FIFA decided that taking your shirt off was punishable with a yellow card, and at times a fine.

Celebrating though you know you'll be punished can be another way for the protagonist to prove his convictions. Batistuta dedicated a goal to an Israeli child who'd been decapitated. He knew he'd be fined for unveiling a picture bearing the child's name, but he paid it very willingly. The fine was part of his gift.

Happiness, without a doubt, is a subjective thing. Some are very secretive in their celebrations, while others, though experiencing something trivial inside, dash off like they're possessed, embracing the manager and knocking over all the water bottles in sight.

Unfortunately for the plurality of passion, football depends on certain rules and regulations. If things get out of hand, if players let their lambada last a little too long, they see yellow. Within FIFA's urbane code, it's looked down on for a player to *exaggerate* any feelings. Since it's down to the ref to decide the sanction, some choreographed dances are punished like crimes of injurious theatricality. The Liverpool player Robbie Fowler was suspended for six matches for his drug-addict celebration: he pretended to sniff the goal line like it was cocaine. The most severe punishments in the game are meted out over what is essentially a question of manners.

Expressiveness has come under controls that are comparable in rigor to anti-doping measures. In its eagerness for players to set a good example, FIFA forgets one of the central aspects of happiness: it always manifests in exceptional ways. But rules are rules, and football players have no choice but to contain their joy in the same way they must hold themselves back if another player spits at them.

"THOU SHALT NOT KILL," AND OTHER EXAMPLES OF INTELLIGENCE

Sports psychologists say you should go out onto the pitch with a cool head. Rise above the heckling of the Milan tifosos, rise above what the Real Madrid forofos think about you, accept it when a perfectly legitimate goal is incorrectly overruled, put up with trash talk, pinches, and bites, as well as insults, the sweat or the saliva of your opposing number; all of these are minimum requirements, at times, if you want to avoid a red card. Truth be told, it isn't easy to stop yourself from being violent when your blood is up and a stadium is rocking. To acquire the internal discipline you need to play the game, you're really better off visiting Tibet than a training session.

The mind of a player is there primarily to keep him in check, to prevent him from murdering the defender who just very nearly broke his tibia. It can also be turned to more creative ends. Let's consider two cerebral attributes that are necessary in the game: the capacity for pleasure and the capacity for mocking others. Great moves, whether by an individual or collectively, have no other motivation than the pleasure of making them happen. When a virtuoso like Hagi or Del Piero plucks a ball out of the air on the tip of their boot, they don't have time to think about where their team is in the table or the professionalism incumbent on them when they don the colors; the impulse is dependent, in equal parts, upon a mastery of your own movements and the knowledge that you are being watched. Great players tease ovations from the crowd and make a mirror for themselves in the applause; acclaim is what they measure themselves by. The writer Osvaldo Soriano once visited the hotel where the Argentine national team was staying, and passed by Maradona without acknowledging him. Could a reporter really ignore this, the greatest dignitary of ball control? No, not when Maradona picked up a mandarin and made a wizardly display of keepy-uppy, right there in the lobby. A smile spread across the face of the portly little diva when he saw he'd impressed the writer.

And what of the mockery of others? Deceit, the ability to trick a player, adds interest to a sport that would die if outcomes were foreseeable. A shimmy of the waist, the deadly pause, and the ball that swerves unpredictably in the air: these surprises are part of the essence of the game. The free kick can even be used to get one over on your opponent.

Usually, players take their heads with them when they leave the stadium. What this means is that they also have to use them in training sessions and on team trips. "Hell is other people," said Sartre, who never even had to go on a team trip, didn't have any children, and wasn't a member of a residents' association. What would he have made of the young men forced to spend longer periods sharing a room with teammates than with their wives?

A player's primary stat is how much he cost. There's little point railing against the transfer market, which is a form of collective madness, nothing more or less; plus, the outlay for Robinho is immediately canceled out when the shirts bearing his name begin flying off the racks. The only thing upon which a value can't be placed in this absurd emporium is the nerves of those directly involved in it. These you can't measure.

The magic of football depends on cunning, a quality that resists all quantification. Suddenly, some slight fear enters the mind of the Ballon d'Or winner, and his shot ends up in Row Z; moments later, some debutant who's yet to sign a permanent contract, whose name nobody knows, forgets about his respect for the legend, and scores the kind of goal that makes people believe in the idea of glory as something improvised.

The war of nerves isn't stipulated in any clause of any contract. It's football's gratuity, the only aspect where the titans of the game remotely resemble those of us who only ever participate in our minds.

3. GOALS AND TIME

In memory of Juan Nuño

Oh, for a club that doesn't cultivate blessed nostalgia.

NELSON RODRIGUES

In "Teoría de los juegos" ("Game Theory"), one of the essays in *Veneración de las astucias* (The Veneration of Cunning), Juan Nuño considers football's temporal specificity. Certain other sports, like baseball and American football, don't have a time limit and can be interrupted by timeouts called by the coaches. Baseball has the most tremendous disdain for chronology: the nine innings can either be over quite quickly, or else last whole days. Like in the *Odyssey*, the goal is to make it home, but how long the journey takes depends entirely on the players' reflexes.

A universal facet of games is the way they suspend the habitual flow of life; under the bright glow of the floodlights, pitches are subject to artificially made schemes and laws. In this capricious universe, football sets itself apart with this trace of unsettling normalcy; there's no way of stopping the passage of time. "A football match is more anxiety-inducing, more dramatic, than any other game," writes Nuño, "for the fact that time runs parallel to time in reality. The strong feelings generated by football are rooted in death, which, each time a human activity is time measured, watches from its hidden vantage." The passage of minutes outside the stadium coincides with that inside it. In American football, an incomplete pass means the clock being stopped; in tennis, when a tiebreak goes to "sudden death," the contest can go on as long as the players remain tied. In the Maracanã, on the other hand, time retains its insistent capacity to zero in on destiny. Not even a 0-0 will necessarily win you extra time. And only in exceptional cases, deciders in a championship or in qualifying, will a game be subject to the shock therapy of penalties or the "golden goal."

The ninety minutes are in a way illusory: they cover the current episode in what is actually a vast genealogy of encounters. In his biography of Boca Juniors, when Martín Caparrós writes, "In 1933, we came in second," in fact there's nothing strange about the statement. Fans truly rooted in their club are integrated into its history. Caparrós talks about something that happened twenty-four years before he was even born, but it has a hold on him with all the ghostly intensity of football's traditions. The time to which the team is subject is the same time to which the spectator is subject.

THE SPEED OF MEMORY

Football nostalgia is always in a hurry. Félix Fernández makes the comment that among the things you lose when you make the move from amateur to pro, the most precious is the "third half," which consists of drinking and remembering; the only thing better than seeing a goal is to play it back. In this period of extra time, passages of play expand and dilate as though Proust were in the dugout.

Memory certainly has the power to make treacherous blows even worse; sometimes its weight is even enough to make a fan retire from the game. "December 19, 1971," a story by the writer Roberto Fontanarrosa, has to do with one such extreme situation. Casale, an old man, has decided never to go and watch his team, Rosario Central, again; he's on the verge of a heart attack, he can't take the wringer they put him through anymore. When his team is playing, he stuffs his ears with cotton wool. He's of the class of fans who will only let someone tell them the score if he has a tranquilizer in hand. But the thing is, Casale is also a legend in his neighborhood; when he went to the stadium, Rosario would win. A group of younger fans, innocent of memory's terrible, lacerating edges, decides to kidnap him and take him to a match, like a lucky charm. The sheer joy of watching his team is too much for his heart, in both senses: he enjoys the match greatly, and when Rosario wins, he meets his double date with destiny, dying in a state of grace after helping his team to victory.

The fanatic who dies goes, as the Ancients put it, "with the majority," which is the destination of all the best fans. If football is an activity that thumbs its nose at death—an imaginary lengthening of the passing of ninety otherwise implacable minutes—it should be assumed that the cheers of everyone who has ever cheered the team on continue to echo around the grounds. In the collection of newspaper columns by the Brazilian writer Nelson Rodrigues, entitled *À Sombra Das Chuteiras Imortais*, he puts forward the following necrological appeal: "No one can miss a Sunday at the Maracanã, and I also include the dead in this call; death exempts no person from their duties to the club." Anyone who has ever heard the roar of a full stadium knows there are more voices than spectators; the ghosts come, too.

Partisan passion may be cumulative, but memories don't all have exactly the same impact; as an adult, you'll never watch a passage of play or an individual move that will electrify you in the same way they would have in your childhood. When you get to be the same age as managers and coaches, and even more so when you're as old as the board of directors, you run through the goals in your memories and find that the most moving ones were scored by players who are by now legends, or are dead, or have Alzheimer's. And then you feel the pull of nostalgia, the idea that the game was always better in the past, which is just as bad in footballing terms as a shattered kneecap; both mean definite retirement.

The museum spectator who finds him- or herself comparing everything with the exploits of the great Garrincha becomes dangerously embittered. Nothing in the present day can ever compare with the unverifiable heroes of the past, who played for no pay and saved penalties with their hands tied behind their backs. Paradise may have been lost, but looking back over the details of the past seems to bring it back to life. What majesty we find in a simple 4-4-2 formation, in referees who wore black, in goalposts made of wood and balls of rawhide! Even the insulting gestures seem wonderful, even someone simulating slitting another player's throat!

This obsession with the mythical past has a thoroughly damaging effect on the present, turning all debuts into betrayals, hurting the obsessive more than anyone else. "You don't know what it used to be like!" cries the outrageous memorizer. The ballerinas with unshaved legs strike him as more attractive than last summer's sylphs.

The story "Esse est percipi" by Jorge Luis Borges and Adolfo Bioy Casares brings together two of football's prime defects: the supremacy of television and the mind tricks of nostalgia. In the story, football is something that has already occurred: the commentators make up the action, deciding for themselves who the scorers were. They have Tulio Savastano, the president of Abasto Juniors, explain the game's true nature: "There's no score, no teams, no matches," he said.

> The stadiums have long since been condemned and are falling to pieces. Nowadays everything is staged on the television and radio. The bogus excitement of the sportscaster—hasn't it ever made you suspect that everything is humbug? The last time a football match was played in Buenos Aires was on June 24, 1937. From that exact moment, football, along with the whole gamut of sports, belongs

to the genre of the drama, performed by a single man in
a booth or by actors in jerseys before the TV cameras.

In the memorable nightmare of Borges and Bioy Casares, football
has become a staged business interest that has been prospering
since St. John's Day, 1937. The story touches on a central vice in
spectators, many of whom treasure the symbolic day of June 24,
the day, according to them, that football died.

When I was young, I was afraid of the men in berets who,
with an extinguished cheroot in their mouth, would come and
regale me with the heroic feats of Isidro Lángara, that hero of
the Basque national team who settled in Mexico because of the
Civil War and whose name entered popular usage. If you got
called a "Lángara" it meant you were crafty, cunning, able to
find your way out of any tight spot.

Though I do my best not to succumb to hopeless nostalgia,
time does take its toll, and the fact is that no goal I witness today
can move me like one I watched thirty-five years in the past. It's
the closing stages of Mexico '70, the infamous Italy vs. Brazil
match, and I hear my father's terrifying words: "In the final,
the team who scores first always loses; that's how it always goes
in World Cups." And I see Pelé, the King, leaping to meet destiny with his forehead, and I see Gérson looking to the sky, his
hands pressed together in prayer, and I see the Estadio Azteca
overflowing with compensatory emotion—in support for Brazil.
"Whoever scores first loses." The dark prophecy injects drama
into the festivities. I'm thirteen, and I've never known my father
to be wrong about anything. But Brazil has Pelé.

Sixteen years later, in the Estadio Azteca in 1986, I was there when Maradona scored his two legendary goals against England, one being the most perfect in the history of illegal goals and the other the most perfect in the history of World Cups. To say I "enjoyed" Pelé's goal would merely be nostalgic resentment; to say I was thrilled by Maradona's goal would be an outrage worthy of a sending off.

Dipping into the football archives is a complicated matter. Even the most forgetful people might need to make multiple lists before going to the supermarket, but they turn into elephants when it comes to the idols of their past. Once, I'd been sitting at dinner with two friends, discussing football for hours, and a man in his seventies came over to us, the wine lighting up his face with a vaguely Magyar tinge. None of us were surprised by the question he put to us: "Okay," he said. "So which one of you can name me the Hungary side from '54?" Apart from Puskás, we had nothing. Stroking his dark gray mustache, adopting a Hussar stance, he recited that tongue twister of a lineup with ease. Did he have a good memory? Who knows, but there was certainly no questioning his passion for the game.

UNENDING TIME:
ONOFRE, THE BRIEF, EVERLASTING GENIUS

To be Mexican and a football addict means, among other things, you have to be a masochist, inflicting on yourself Thursdays of pain for which there aren't any resurrection Sundays. What would become of us if we were stripped of this turbulent melodrama? At one point in the fifteenth-century Spanish romance *Tirant the White*, the main character gets a clip around the ear from his father, apparently for no reason. The father explains: the surprise blow would mean the son never forgot the moment in question. Wounds set the clock.

In the 1970s, my generation learned the names of two bones, the tibia and the fibula, after Alberto Onofre fractured both in the final training session before the World Cup. The midfielder slipped and fell into Juan Manuel Alejándrez. It hardly rained during the World Cup itself; it had to rain before, as a way of refining the tragedy.

The son of a lathe turner, he took numerous beatings in the name of his passion for the game, and when he joined Guadalajara he was embarrassed to take his clothes off because of all the bruises. He overcame the kind of adversity you'd associate with characters played by Mexican Golden Age actor Pedro Infante, and in the 1969–70 season he played such brilliant football that you have to turn to two Striped Goats legends to describe it: he initiated moves like Benjamín Galindo, able to send the play left or right masterfully, and he could finish them off as elegantly as Héctor Hernández. At twenty-two, he was the on-field general that the Mexican national team had never had before, and would never have again.

Any fan of my generation will remember the doom of losing our best player on the eve of hosting the World Cup. Not for the first time, bad luck was at home. An ambulance, with its own convoy, took the injured player to the hospital. The surgeon wanted to put him in a gown, but, to top off the drama, Onofre asked to be operated on as he was, wearing the Mexico strip. He would never wear it again.

Though I'll never forget the scene, the wonderful book by Agustín del Moral Tejeda, *Un crack mexicano: Alberto Onofre* (A Mexican Maestro: Alberto Onofre), paints it in greater detail. With exacting sincerity, he parallels the failures on the pitch and in the newspaper rooms with those of the broken-down player. And yet there's a bitter lesson offered by the book's main character: "My story is, if you like, tragic, but his, I'm sorry, is truly pathetic." With this as his unexpected premise, he constructs a double tale, vilifying at the same time as performing the essential role of bearing witness to Onofre. What is a chronicler if not the shadow cast by a hero on his way out?

Like so many other transitory figures, he didn't keep a record of his great feats. A girlfriend cut out all the articles written about Onofre in the 1970s, and this was the material that Moral Tejeda used to weave his tale. This is how we're able to go back to the present moment of the header Onofre scored past Rafael Puente to win the Goats the league title before the World Cup. Ramón Márquez, a journalist for *Excélsior*, wrote this of the goal: "Alberto Onofre, in ecstasy, put his head in his hands, standing stock still until his teammates arrived and buried him at the bottom of a dramatic human pyramid in the Atlante goalmouth." The scene captures something of the mystery of sporting moments: the protagonist, unable to be his own witness, needs others to react before he can comprehend what he's done. At its best, the sports report becomes a kind of internal mirror: in having his story told, the hero of the moment discovers himself.

Moral Tejeda waited thirty-three years to recount the moment that defined an era in Mexican football. Onofre would never be the same man again. There were complications with the operation, but, more importantly, he never overcame the trauma of being defeated before a World Cup ball was even kicked. To what extent did his environment inhibit his recovery? American culture loves to see a comeback: even more important than winning is doing it again, against the odds, as with Joe Montana in the Super Bowl, after he had broken his back, coming back to lead "The Drive," the greatest ever time-reversing offense in history. Onofre complained, rightly, about the lack of psychological support he was given. The executives of the game, so fawning in the run-up to the World Cup, didn't come to see him, and the fans, predisposed to losing, just accepted that their greatest player had vanished into the keen midday sun. Nothing sums up Mexican football better than a prodigy who had the world at his feet but didn't last the course.

In *Un crack mexicano*, as Onofre goes back over what happened to him, he seems sad, which is logical enough, but the bitter knife of vindication is lacking. And the story has another exceptional aspect to it: the fall also put an end to the career of Juan Manuel Alejándrez, the Cruz Azul defender. It was chance rather than intention that put him in the wrong place, but he was there, and he played his part in the drama. The hesitancy that clouded his mind is impossible to judge. He was a nailed-on starter, and after missing out on the World Cup, his star waned. Was his suffering worse than Onofre's, a depression with nothing to show for it, one measured out in episodes (has been, no longer is), and one that a full fracture would have broken more cleanly?

Time keeps on replaying this particular move. Onofre and Alejándrez both live in Guadalajara. When they meet at some veteran's match or other, neither of them mentions what happened in 1970. Something threw them into one another—"It was the weapons, not the men, who fought," as Borges wrote. It's a story that evokes an abiding, changeless, inescapable something: the hero that never was; the accidental villain; a duel in which there were only losers.

Perhaps, under other circumstances, one rainy Thursday, someone will be Onofre again, and someone else Alejándrez.

BARBOSA: THE MAN WHO DIED TWICE

On occasion, a footballer's accomplishments on the pitch are so comprehensive that the life outside of it seems like just hazy posterity. The clock of reputation doesn't always adjust to that of biology.

Moacyr Barbosa, the first black goalkeeper to play for Brazil, died on April 8, 2000. Some thirty mourners attended his funeral, and his coffin was draped in the colors of the now-dissolved club Ypiranga. Just before the coffin was carried to the cemetery, one of the Vasco da Gama executives removed an Ypiranga flag from the grave.

In a country where footballers take on the status of semi-divine beings, Barbosa's send-off was more befitting of a ghost. It made little difference that the keeper had won five Rio league titles and a Sudamérica title with Vasco da Gama. His tragic fate was sealed in a moment from which he never recovered.

It happened on July 16, 1950. There were two hundred thousand fans in the recently opened Maracanã—a record in the history of the game—for the World Cup final between Brazil and Uruguay. The rules in those days meant the home side only had to draw to win the trophy. The Brazilian newspapers had already prepared the next day's victorious headlines. Even Jules Rimet, the inventor of the World Cup, had prepared a speech eulogizing the skill of Rio-born players and the affectionate warmth of Brazil's public. The words never made it out of his pocket.

Over half a century later, the match remains etched in the memories of millions of Brazilians. Even those who didn't see it know the episode that brought the country to a standstill. Brazil went ahead first, through Friaça, who at that point thought his side had won their first cup. When Schiaffino scored for Uruguay, the fervor in the stadium was dampened without dying down altogether; a draw made the achievement less epic, but it would still do. A free kick ended up deciding the game. Ghiggia crossed the ball, and Barbosa—a keeper who had cut his teeth against the most sophisticated attackers on the planet—came to collect it. The subjectivity of heroes doesn't always have a great deal to do with reality. Brazil's last man gathered the ball and fell, relieved, onto the sacred grass of the Maracanã. He'd saved the shot, he was sure. The silence that fell returned him to the moment and to a horrified nation, the two hundred thousand mute spectators looking on. The ball was in the back of the net. Uruguay 2, Brazil 1.

In the Pelé film, this is the moment when the young lion grabs the radio and bashes it, sobbing. Brazil lost, at home, bucking all prognostication. Pelé's story would go on to be—to a great degree—one of rectification. The thousand-plus goals he scored were destined to make up for the one that Moacyr Barbosa was unable to keep out.

In his story "A Minute's Absence," François Bott recounts the sad fate of Luis Arconada, the Spain goalkeeper, in the 1984 European Championship final against France. Though Platini's France side was the clear favorite, victory was handed to them in the most unlikely manner, with a shot that would have been saved on any school playground. As though fulfilling the prophecy contained in his name, Arconada, or "hell of a goal," let in a weak shot that only became significant because of his error.

With Barbosa it was different; he didn't commit an obvious mistake like Arconada, but rather let destiny take his eye off the ball. He thought he was doing the right thing, before suddenly finding himself in a world where he was the villain.

The main character in Bott's story is Antoine Mercier, a tried and tested goalkeeper who had saved many a difficult shot, only to be undone by one that should have been easy to keep out. The key moment comes when the number 1 makes the same mistake as so many other keepers: he thinks deeply for a moment, becomes distracted, observing his life in slow motion. For one joyful moment, he lapses into abstraction, wandering back down the labyrinth of memory lane, cutting himself off from the present situation—perhaps not so lush but far more pressing—and with it his shot-stopping role. It's an insipid shot; he should save it easily, but he's immersed in his "minute's absence."

Like Mercier, Barbosa lapsed into his inner world before coming to ground. Curiously, unlike his French colleague, his happy moment wasn't due to a pleasant sentimental episode but to the misguided belief that he'd done the right thing. His sadness was exacerbated by the second of joy that preceded it. Barbosa came unstuck in a moment of pure wishful thinking, and then he realized it, and that made it all the harder. "A whole career, and a whole life, destroyed by a minute's absence," as François Bott put it.

The tragic goalkeeper of the Maracanã went on playing until 1962, and even won a number of trophies with Vasco da Gama. In a magisterial piece of sports journalism, Eric Nepomuceno wrote the following: "Ever the efficient keeper, elegant, agile, with an elastic frame that got down quickly to smother any shot, he nonetheless committed the worst of errors: failing to keep out the one shot that mattered." In *Football in Sun and Shadow*, Eduardo Galeano paints his portrait thus: "When it was time to select the best goalkeeper of the 1950 World Cup, journalists voted unanimously for Barbosa. Without a doubt, Barbosa was the best keeper in the country, a man with springs in his legs whose calm self-assurance filled the entire team with confidence."[*] And yet his prestige among the experts could do nothing to win him back the affection of the supporters.

The bigots—always near at hand—accused him of lacking the levelheadedness of white players. Brazil's first black goalkeeper had not only to suffer defeat but also aspersions on his race.

Barbosa retired on a pension of eighty-five dollars a month, an amount later increased by Vasco da Gama. Night after night he dreamed of that disastrous goal, and was regularly excoriated in public. A woman in the street once pointed him out to her young son: "This is the man," she said, "who made a country cry."

A documentary was made in 1993 on English television, in preparation for USA '94. The production team had the idea of taking Barbosa to visit the Brazil squad, but Brazil's national coach, Mário Zagallo, refused; he was worried Barbosa would be an ambassador of misfortune and infect his players with his bad luck. Asked about the incident, Barbosa, a desolate look in his eye, said that in Brazil the maximum prison sentence for any crime was thirty years, yet he was the only person serving a life sentence.

Barbosa's wife Clotilde died in 1997. He outlived her by three years, sufficient time to verify just how lonely he was. Finally, at seventy-nine years of age, the keeper came to Earth for the last time.

His first death had been half a century earlier, in a sun-kissed goalmouth in the Maracanã. Let us return, through imagination's trance, to Ghiggia crossing, the keeper coming to claim

---

[*]   Translation by Mark Fried.

it. His hands alight on the ball, diverting it slightly. Let's pause, forever, on Moacyr Barbosa's airborne lunge. The young black keeper is up above the ground, feeling the ball in his hands, thinking he's saved his side. He's happy now. There, up on his own in the silence of the as-yet undecided, in the instant we really ought to remember.

WAYS OF STOPPING TIME

Memorious posterity gets plenty of chances to justify itself in a sport where everyone is fighting against the clock, and where careers come and go in a flash. Michel Platini begins his book, *Ma vie comme un match* (*My Life Is Like a Ball Game*), with this confession from beyond the grave: "I died at the age of thirty-two, on May 17, 1987: the day I retired from the game." Memory is the only hereafter for a retired footballer, either securing his place as a legend or refusing to pass him the ball.

There used to be a brash Mexican commentator who always used to conclude his broadcasts with a defiant statement: "There's my reputation for you; I leave it here for you to destroy." Very few would wish to leave their fate in the hands of the public, and the player fights, with at times pitiful resistance, to prolong the match days upon which their reputation will rest. As Nelson Rodrigues pointed out, all very good players who are over the hill (over thirty) "suffer from the now." One morning the pitch seems suddenly huge, the goal a distant mirage. But the main threat to the veteran is not his own decline as much as the numbers on the bench announcing the arrival of a new player. Jorge Valdano took the unenviable decision to remove Emilio Butragueño from the pitch—with the consent of the Real Madrid supporters—and later spelled out the drama better than anyone: "Who was this Raúl to take Butragueño's shirt, to steal his headlines, to muscle in on his place in people's affections? Easy. Raúl was the march of time, which in its own special way was again the winner."

As a way of immortalizing their heroes, sports in the United States place emphasis on their absence by an irreversible gesture: their shirt is retired. For San Francisco, number 16 will never play again—or, put better, it will only ever play in the minds of those who care to recall the deadly precision of Joe Montana's passes.

Some teams organize themselves around the past in such a way that it becomes their very reason for being. Over the course of several trophyless decades, Universidad de Chile took shelter in a song evoking the championship-winning "Blue Ballet" side: "We'll be back, we'll be back/Back again/We'll be great/Great like the Ballet." Winning the league in 1994 was like a formidable return to their past.

Putting the past to one side for a moment (or for ninety minutes), let us return to the reality of the passing of time in a match. Is there any way to make the minutes proceed differently? Time-outs in basketball and American football are used to plan moves and to take the sting out of a game when an opponent is gaining the upper hand. In the beautiful game, only an operatic fall can prompt a referee to stop the clock. The club's most humble staff member, the doctor, suddenly becomes a strategist, coming into the suspended game, opening the kit bag and, like a witch, bringing out the *magic spray*, the sponge, the good-luck cloth. In spite of the fact everyone, including the ref, knows that the blow was on the lower half of the player's body, he gets a rub on the solar plexus, a bit of leg stretching so he can regain his breath, and, in the most sophisticated instances, a bit of something daubed on the eyebrow.

The funereal whistle blasts—peep peep peep!—and like a judicial procedure, the match offers obits and stats by way of a settlement: supporters turn their short-lived heroes into immortals, and a new crease appears on the trainer's brow. The game enters into that zone of deferred promises; that which has passed is now that which is to come, the happy antidote for the time-sick, those of us who line the stands.

THE PECULIARITY
OF BEING TWO-LEGGED

Two things make football difficult for me.
One is my left leg. The other is my right.

ROBERTO FONTANARROSA

THE OTHER LEG

One of football's great enigmas is players having two legs. Normally they only make use of one in actually contacting the ball and become so one-footed that the other leg becomes nothing but a shadow, just something to stand on.

When a right-footed player is forced to use his left, the result is more like a streamer than a shot. "He used his standing leg!" the TV commentator will exclaim.

Many are the players that seem straight out of *Treasure Island*, pirates whose lower limbs have been snacked on by sharks.

Some great players have been just as good with the left and right foot, and equally as skilled at heading or even controlling the ball with a shoulder. And yet this tends to be more what you get from circus performers than footballers.

When I'm driving my daughter to school we often see a keepy-uppy artist at one of the stop signals, juggling different-sized balls with all different parts of his body, not excluding his nose. Does this make him a footballer? I fear it does not.

It's essential to have good ball control, but it's only of use if that control can be put to the good of the specific mission in hand—passing the ball, creating a goal. Most top players orientate themselves in unusual ways, such that when they receive the ball they're in a position to pull off a trick or two; this is where talk of a player's "correct profile" stems from. A decent defender won't look to stop a striker from moving altogether—they know that's impossible—but they will try to make it difficult for them to receive the ball in their preferred position.

Why do players allow themselves to be subject to such limitations? Wouldn't it be better to learn to control the ball like a sea lion does, nudging it forward for themselves with their noses? The history of football is a history of stubbornness, though, as shown by the fact that the greats have not been versatile, but brilliant, absolutely perfect, at one specific skill.

Football is also a Homeric activity: each person offers a specific something. As Hector is the horse tamer, and as Achilles is swift of foot, players focus on the virtue that sets them apart, whether it be scoring, heading, winning the ball back, bicycle kicks, passing, or lightning-fast counterattacks.

The football player knows, like the protagonist in the Ramuz story *The Soldier's Tale*, famously put to music by Stravinsky, that "one happy thing is every happy thing." He must pick the form his joy will take. A magnificently difficult thing when you've got two legs to choose from.

Players who combine great strength with great ability, like Didier Drogba, and players who can operate equally well off either foot, like Xavi, seem intent on flouting the fidelity to a single skill that football seems to demand. But even such players who do everything well have one skill, something unique and untransferable, that they do best.

The story of man's evolution begins with *Homo erectus* learning to walk on two feet. And in the same way that art exists in order to correct nature, football shows that a genius only needs one leg.

LEFTISTS, LEFTIES

The state of the world today is such that you'd be forgiven for thinking that the football pitch is the final refuge for anyone with left leanings.

Lefties are traditionally the mavericks and speed merchants who give the impression of playing on the other side of the looking glass.

In the days when shirt numbers corresponded with players' positions, and therefore their psychology, "11" meant "left wing." In football, the last in the line is uneven, the iconoclast within a system that chose to be decimal.

Football has made us used to a certain biological mystery: the left foot begins life more specialized than the right. Left footers are more often virtuosos, and often particularly bad with their right foot. A model of ruggedness and substance, Martín Palermo managed to become equally skilled with either foot but never excellent with either.

Sometimes you don't need to double up on resources. For Messi or Maradona to be as good with their right foot as their left would just be excessive. In their cases it's just surprising they have another foot at all.

Every so often Javier Marías writes about the discrimination suffered by the Left, and he knows what he's talking about because he writes, and smokes his cigarettes, with his left hand. Cases abound of children being forced to write with their "correct" hand—not the left.

Football can't be said to openly discriminate against those who light up the pitch's endmost corner, like the Portuguese Paulo Futre, or those who patrol that side of the pitch, like Roberto Carlos. Others, like Hugo Sánchez, reject their natural habitat. He was put out on the left for a time, because his left foot was his strongest, but his great skill was shooting inside the area, not operating outside it. If he'd been right-footed no one would ever have thought to play him on the wing.

People fixate on left footers and want to place limits on them. How many left footers can a single team bear? A team with only right footers would be boring but tolerable, whereas if there were any more than three lefties, the coach would have a heart attack. Will there ever come a time when a team features left footers only?

I once had a conversation with an Argentine friend about Fernando Redondo, a sublime player with the look of a tragic

Prince Valiant about him, who had an injury-blighted career, and whose participation in the Argentina national side was limited because he refused to cut his hair. My friend reminded me of a character in a book by Juan Ruiz de Alarcón who referred to himself thusly: "My name is Redondo, but make no mistake, I'm sharp."

And I was praising the winger when my friend disagreed thus: "He's too left-footed." A strange criticism, I thought, given that we were discussing a sport in which the greats are perfect at one thing only, like Gerd Müller, who could volley better than anyone, Oliver Bierhoff with his great header, Hugo Sánchez, whose bicycle kicks were unsurpassed, David Beckham with his free kicks, and Maradona with that one ability: to make fools of the entire opposing team. And yet some connoisseurs would still say that a player can be too left-footed.

People who love regularity and eternal spring mistrust rain if it wasn't forecast and any unexpected surge up the left. And even more, any artificer who makes the whole pitch seem "left field."

Guardians of the unpredictable, those who do not salute with their right hand out of instinct but because they accept a world in which they are in the minority, are also confirmation of the rare thing that is originality.

The great Brazil side that triumphed at Mexico '70 had Rivellino as their number 11. He admired Pelé, but knew that the King lacked a certain singular feature that would make him perfect. One day he went up to him and said: "You'd have liked to be left-footed, wouldn't you?"

To which the King didn't respond.

THE DEATHS OF OTHERS

CONSPIRACY

During the 2006 World Cup in Germany the film everybody was talking about was *The Lives of Others*, the main character in which is a Stasi agent in the German Democratic Republic (GDR). He's spying on a couple from one of the GDR's circles of intellectuals, but he finds himself increasingly drawn into their lives.

The "furtive education" of the spy, who comes to empathize with the people he's following, represents a reversal of the tensions in socialist Germany. According to some estimates, one in three people was an unofficial Stasi informer, the point of this whistle-blowing culture being to pick up on dissidence as it was still forming, before it might crystallize in some actual deed.

I lived in East Germany from 1981 to 1984, and met people who lost out on internships and jobs because they were suspected as potential dissidents. The evidence against them could be as slight as the presence of a Western magazine in a desk drawer or some chance encounter with a foreigner.

And now those who were spied on are able to go back over the archives. A bold decision on the part of a society that wanted to avoid repeating the post-Nazi pact of silence. Some said it would only open Pandora's box to allow huge numbers of people to look back over so many unpleasant episodes. Learning that your loved ones informed on you is no easy thing to take.

I, dossier number XV 1790/73, was among the millions who were kept under observation—in my case because of my work at the Mexican Embassy in Berlin. I subsequently looked up the secret files they had on me—out of curiosity, but also hoping to discover what was so interesting about my life in those years. Perhaps my shadow life would turn out to have been better than my real one. Predictably enough, I failed to find any of the intricate plots that filled the four-thousand-page dossier they kept on the ice skater Katarina Witt, or the symposia of paranoia that made Günter Grass's folder so bulky. And yet, meager though the information on me was, it remains testament to the irrationality of a system that guaranteed automatic resentment from the populace.

The secret police were no strangers to football; they even had their own team: BFC Dynamo. Paradoxical though it may have been for thousands of fans to go and watch a team comprising secret agents, Dynamo wasn't out of place in a league where, after all, the army and the police force also fielded sides.

Germany '06 brought to mind the story of a footballer that the Stasi kept files on. Lutz Eigendorf had defected to West Germany in 1979, where he joined the Rhineland club Kaiserslautern. The head of the Stasi, Erich Mielke, was extremely displeased at the impression this gave of the new socialist dawn and put plans in motion for a long and drawn-out revenge.

The fact Mielke loved hunting seems almost superfluous. He stalked Eigendorf for four years, in addition to harassing his wife and young daughter, who had stayed behind in the GDR. The footballer tried in vain to get them brought over the border. In an attempt to access the family's most intimate secrets, the Stasi even sent in a hired lothario to seduce his wife. Utterly fed up and convinced he was being watched constantly, Eigendorf decided to opt out of the game by changing sides; he joined team Alcoholic. His mind had always been disposed to evasion, and he then took up another new hobby: flying. Getting away was the only thing on the mind of the besieged striker.

On March 5, 1983, he went to the bar where he was a regular, had a few drinks, and said an early good night. He had a flying lesson the following day. He drove away along a back road, which at one point passed through a forest. Suddenly there was a dazzling light up ahead as a car turned on its unusually bright headlights. Eigendorf lost control and crashed into a tree, dying in the act.

Minutes to Stasi meetings have revealed that the accident was no accident; a shadowy clock was measuring out the footballer's every minute on Earth. At twenty-six years of age, Lutz Eigendorf paid the price for his defection. A man who vaulted defenders with ease had not succeeded in evading history.

ASSASSINATION

René Higuita committed the sin of going to "The Cathedral"—
not to Mass but to the jail where Pablo Escobar, the drug lord and
former owner of Colombian sides Independiente and Atlético
Nacional de Medellín, was being held.

In a country of huge inequality, Escobar's popularity rested on
his philanthropy and his support of certain clubs. Proceeds from
cocaine went into repainting the chalk lines at the stadiums of
struggling sides, and that was how the record-breaking Nacional
side also got going. In 1989, under the management of Francisco
Maturana, the green-and-whites won the Copa Libertadores, a
feat no Colombian side had ever managed before.

When Escobar attended matches he gave the impression
of an honest salesman. He was a brutal assassin, but received
preferential treatment in all business dealings and from the
Colombian Football Federation.

And when he fell out of favor and was locked up, Higuita
showed loyalty. The keeper who specialized in coming and col-
lecting crosses had gone too far this time: he visited the prison,
had a hand in the escape of an inmate, and was himself arrested.
That left him unavailable to play at USA '94.

The Colombian side went into that World Cup having won
twenty-five of their last twenty-six matches. Carlos Valderrama
loped around as though he were taking his siesta at the same time
he was pulling off miracles, Asprilla and Valencia scored goals of
Brazilian brilliance, and Andrés Escobar brought Beckenbauer
to mind with his gentleman-of-the-pitch demeanor.

A freak occurrence had been their downfall in Italia '90. Higuita went on a dribble with the ball outside his area, only to be tackled by the thirty-eight-year-old Roger Milla, who helped himself to an early retirement present.

Their victories in World Cup qualifying were the victories of the kind of sides not accustomed to winning, and they played with the kind of originality you don't get when three points are expected. They beat Argentina 5-0 in River Plate's Estadio Monumental and ended up being applauded by their opponents.

With their frizzy hairdos and big beards, they resembled pirates in search of some good rum to drink. The country's president, César Gaviria, followed the team wherever it played, hoping to underline the fact that his nation was more than just cocaine and semiautomatics; the country with the twentieth century's most scrutinized passport had become charismatic.

The national side didn't lack imagination; reality was superfluous. Other drug lords went on to copy Escobar, "El Mexicano" taking over Millonarios and Miguel Rodríguez taking over América de Cali. Money laundering and betting syndicates were other legacies of the Colombian triumph.

Just before the World Cup, the three-year-old son of one of the players was kidnapped: a foretelling of the tragedies to come in the competition. Against Romania the substitute keeper let in a Hagi shot from fifty yards out, and the match ended 3-1 to Romania. The team's fate was sealed against the USA. Rarely has a match been played in such an unbearably tense atmosphere. Maturana was late showing up in the dressing room, and when he did arrive he was in tears. He'd received death threats that had included demands to not start a certain player. He obeyed, knowing the danger it meant.

And it was a judgment, not a game, that then took place. The scoreboard was as good as a sentence. In trying to clear a ball, the impeccable Andrés Escobar scored an own goal. His look as he gazed at his feet was unforgettable: the look of a condemned man.

When he went back to Medellín he didn't want to hide, and tried to carry on with his life as normal. He was murdered outside a nightclub. A girl accompanied him to the hospital, holding his hand and whispering sweet nothings to him. The Gentleman pretended to listen, showing that when Colombian heroes triumph, it's only imaginary.

HEART ATTACK

Nothing is harder to understand than the heart. Cardiologists and poets know it equally well. Time can be measured in heartbeats, but heartbeats themselves are immeasurable. This essential uncertainty fed into an unforgettable drama in August 2007, with the death of the Sevilla player Antonio Puerta.

A twenty-two-year-old collapsing on a football pitch, without warning, with no apparent cause, just shows the precariousness of life. And that it should happen to someone experiencing the highs of a team that has just won the Spanish Super Cup is a reminder that all happiness is accompanied by its potential opposite, the ashes and dust that await us all.

Sportspeople of today are more like martyrs to physical punishment than symbols of well-being. Once athletes retire they begin to suffer certain aches and pains unknown to those of us who haven't been elbowed and kicked for a living.

The night before a match, a professional basketball player dines with ice packs strapped to his knees. In the case of footballers, the ice goes on the ankles.

Sports science has begun devising energy cocktails that come within an inch of doping. Any person who relies on their body to compete is more than happy to go along with the superstitions of the treatment table: for a striker who's missed three sitters in a single match it's a no-brainer to put his blood in a centrifuge. And let's remember Ronaldo's blurry vision in the final of France '98 after he'd had injections more suited to a racehorse.

Athletes' short careers, and their astronomical wages, seem like justifications for the way they abuse their bodies. They have to take part in more and more competitions all the time, and coaches are forever on the lookout for ways to utilize their best players without ruining them for later in the season. There is much talk in modern football of squad rotation, though it goes against the psychology of true competitors: if the team runs out three times in a week, they want to play every time.

Did Puerta have a heart attack because too much was being asked of his body? As the heart is obscure, the speculations have been wide ranging. Puerta had undergone some very demanding physical tests a few days before his death, and he passed with flying colors. After his collapse he received expert attention and all the support a person could need in the Virgen del Rocío

Hospital. His case doesn't point to a problem that had gone unnoticed, but rather to a job that makes huge demands of an organism without this seeming to be a problem. Training leads to a kind of fatigue that no one notices.

The name Antonio Puerta, straightforward, easy on the ear, was that of a local idol; his bond with Sevilla was unusual in these times of globe-hopping transfers. The pain caused by his death and the scenes of open grief in the streets brought to mind the *Semana Santa* processions, particularly the Virgin's Solitude section, when the city is brought into full cognizance of the loss of the Son.

The number 16 he wore has taken on an almost religious symbolism. Entrance number 16 at Sevilla's stadium has turned into a candle-filled shrine, and even fans of Real Betis, Sevilla's archenemy, had the number 16 printed on their green-and-white shirts. These moving shows of respect for the opposition demonstrate that it takes terrible misfortune for the game's tribal animosities to be put aside.

The tragedy of Antonio Puerta recalled other incomprehensibly sad moments in the game. Like Pedro Berruezo, another Sevilla player, going down during a 1973 game as though struck by lightning. Like Puerta he was expecting a child, and like Puerta he had a history of collapses. Thirty-four years later the scene would repeat itself. Some parallels are utterly confounding.

Another thing that doesn't make sense is the debt teams owe to past players. A team can be on fire and then lose at a stadium because their club has failed to win there for twenty-four years. How do such hoodoos function? Players who weren't born at the time of that first, fateful defeat play as though they were, and still are, there. The Brazilian writer Nelson Rodrigues had the answer: death is no obstacle, he tells us, to people's responsibilities to their club. The match-day eleven and the people in the stands are a minority compared to the ghosts. Every person who has ever played for and shouted on their team is present; a team is as great as its specters.

When they won the Super Cup, Sevilla showed the value of togetherness in this team sport. In their triumph, their fallen are also on their side.

Antonio Puerta has the ball.

MAGIC NUMBER 10

TEN IS A KEY NUMBER for a species that uses its fingers to count. The decimal system allows time to be measured with the hands.

Logically enough, in football the roundest number is bestowed on the great craftsmen and generals, the players who dictate the way their teams play.

Though officially taking up position in midfield and further forward, a number 10's magnetism is felt the length and breadth of the pitch.

Cases like Maradona and Pelé aside, the 10 doesn't tend to score as often as the center forward, but covers more ground and sees more of the ball. A complex team move goes down more exactly in the memory than a wonderful finish.

The far-reaching influence of a number 10 is clear to see, but his main virtue is to improve those around him—the players who do everything they can to get him to pass to them. If the opposition can keep the strategist quiet, it's like death to the team's brain. The true significance of the number on this player's back is how many other players depend on him.

All lists are arbitrary. Mine includes only players I've seen in action. There have been other superlative players in this position, but not many.

Millions of feet have kicked footballs. Only a select few have cast a spell on it.

DIDI: THE FIRST

The best player at the 1958 World Cup was Waldyr Pereira, also known as Didi and baptized by the commentator and playwright Nelson Rodrigues—Brazilian football's prime mythographer—as the Ethiopian Prince.

When he ran up to take a penalty, he'd always stop just before making contact. It was this pause—the celebrated "little stop"—that would beat the keeper. His other trick, his "dry leaf" free kick, was harder to imitate: he'd kick the ball very high into the air, as though the goal were up in the stands, but apply such spin that it dipped goalward while at the same time swerving viciously and unpredictably. The shot foretold the autumn of the goalkeeper.

Few players have ever oozed such calm as the Prince. After Brazil's first goal in the final in Sweden, he sauntered back to the center circle with the ball under his arm. So serene was he, so imperturbable, that the message was clear: you hurry, you lose.

If his teammates ever demanded he inject some pace into the game, he'd usually respond by saying, "We're better than them, no need to rush." Convinced that time favors the best team, he played as though the clock was all in the mind.

Like so many heroes, misfortune drove him on. After getting in a fight at the age of fourteen, he was left in a wheelchair and was told he would have to have a leg amputated. He said to himself that if he ever regained the power of his legs, he'd use them to reinvent the world, but also that he'd do so without any worries, demonstrating that the greatest virtuosity consists in doing things simply.

He was the greatest player ever to don the colors of the Brazil club side Fluminense, and in 1950 scored the first-ever goal at the Maracanã. He won the Brazilian league with Botafogo in 1957 and fulfilled his promise to cross Rio on foot—with preternatural calm, naturally. "Timing is at the King's discretion," goes the saying, and the Prince would time his runs into the box for when he judged it appropriate.

Didi won the World Cup for a second time in Mexico and played out the rest of his career with the Mexican club side Red Sharks Veracruz.

With his magisterial elegance, he made us believe his feats couldn't be reproduced. A talented young player emerged in 1958 and said the following words to the press: "I'm nothing next to Didi. I'll never be anywhere near the level of Didi. He's my idol, my only reference point. The first football stickers I ever bought were of him." And the name of the sixteen-year-old novice who worshiped the Prince of Calm?

Edson Arantes do Nascimento.

PELÉ: THE KING

When Nelson Rodrigues saw Pelé play, he knew he had to come up with a nickname to better the one he'd given Didi. It was March 25, 1958, and at the time he wrote that royalty is a state of being. Who manifested it on the field of play? The commentator's eye was drawn to a teenager who had just finished off a bewitching move. "To score a goal like this," wrote Rodrigues, "you need more than mere skill. You need something extra: the total self-confidence, certainty, and optimism that made Pelé so impossible to defend against. What I mean to say is that his greatest virtue is his absolute immodesty. The way he is above everything and above everyone finally awes even the ball itself." Rodrigues had seen the man who would be the King.

Slavery was only abolished in Brazil in 1888. Edson Arantes was a member of the third generation of free blacks, and changed the country's vision of itself.

His father once caught him smoking as a teenager. "Bad idea to smoke if you want to make it as a professional footballer," he said. "But if you're going to do it, here's some money for tobacco. I don't want you going around begging for it."

The King acted with the dignity of those who feel they mustn't ask for anything, beginning with the cigarette money from his father. He never touched cigarettes again, which came as a surprise to the greatest party animal ever to grace the game, George Best. "What kind of King are you," he asked, "if you don't drink or smoke?"

We can talk about a select elite of greats in modern football, but only one King. Edson Arantes was the perfect dramatist—even his goal celebration (a spring-heeled leap, arm aloft) was spectacular. Three World Cups, over a thousand goals. He could drop his shoulder and leave a defender on the floor, and he could vault a six-foot Russian. He turned physical power into a way of setting the rhythm. He combined Didi's class with Jesse Owens's love of top gear.

He made his debut at the age of fifteen for Santos, and his brilliant career lasted two decades, a reign never to be repeated.

As well as the goals he scored, he made other ludicrous attempts that didn't end up as goals, but that have nonetheless gone down as pieces of art for art's sake.

BOBBY CHARLTON: BACK FROM THE DEAD

The country that produced Shakespeare deserved a ghost to settle a score with destiny. A plane carrying the Manchester United squad crashed in 1958, killing eight players. Bobby Charlton was one of the few Busby Babes to survive, and went on to play the game with the gossamer subtlety of a player who's done preseason training in the afterlife.

His through passes defined the character of the English game, one that pertains to this day in the Premier League. He wouldn't pass to a player, but to the gap into which he expected him to run.

The goals he scored resembled noble acts. The goalkeeper would watch them fly past with all the surprise of the swordsman who falls while admiring his rival.

Charlton holds the record for most goals in both the Man Utd strip and that of England. He led the national team to the World Cup in 1966 and was made a knight—a title he already held on the field of play.

He's also partly responsible for the invention of yellow and red cards. England were facing Argentina at Wembley when the German referee Rudolf Kreitlein sent off the away team's captain, Antonio Rattín, because of a linguistic mix-up. (The Argentine had merely asked for the official to explain a decision, and the ref thought he was insulting him.) Later in the game, he cautioned Charlton, who made as though he didn't understand something. ("If you don't know what they've said," he's on record as saying, "you don't need to *do* what they've said.") The English midfield general acted disdainfully toward the ref who had been so impudent as to give his team an unfair advantage. Ashamed by the helping hand they'd been given, he simply ignored the man in charge.

At the end of the chaotic encounter, the linesman, a man named Ken Aston, thought it through on his journey home. He realized that it hadn't been possible for the ref to punish Charlton without justifying himself to the stadium. So he came up with the idea of notifying players of their situation with cards, and the resource was given its first outing at the next World Cup, Mexico '70.

True to his belief that football ought to be pleasing on the eye, Charlton baptized Old Trafford "The Theatre of Dreams."

The Bard's most celebrated stage direction comes in *Hamlet*: "Enter Ghost." The eight players who died in the air disaster were avenged by a pallid player who came back from a place of no return, showing that, truly, man is built from such stuff as dreams are made on.

OVERATH: THE PILOT

Though Lothar Matthäus took part in five World Cups (the only outfield player ever to do so), he didn't have the class, or the solidity of character, of Wolfgang Overath, who played his entire club career for FC Cologne and turned out in the Germany side of the Beckenbauer years.

In *The Man without Qualities*, Robert Musil makes the comment that Austria developed the greatest bureaucracy the world had ever seen; this brought about a value system that obviated surprises. In the Austro-Hungarian Empire it was very unlikely that a cretin would be mistaken for a genius, but not that unusual for a genius to be mistaken for a cretin.

On occasion, the work of football analysts is like this. They know how to discard the obviously poor players, but have a harder time properly weighing up an artist who isn't especially showy. Overath belongs to the select group of understated rhetoricians.

He provided the calm thinking for an epic Germany side that dominated the world game for eight years. They lost the 1966 final in Wembley to a "ghost goal," took part in the "game of the century" against Italy at Mexico '70, and came close at Germany '74, only to lose to the GDR.

In a national side that pitted itself against destiny, the axis of the team was a left footer—a measured, prudent number 10. If you isolate the moves he orchestrated, it's impossible to guess the score at the time; he went around placidly seeking the right pass. When they played England in Mexico '70, during extra time you can see that his socks aren't pulled up: the only signal that something out of the ordinary is going on.

When Günter Netzer came on the scene, he started challenging for the shirt, which turned Overath into an even better player. In a very German way, the rivals discovered that competition was a reason to be friends, and a means for demanding more of oneself.

Between 1966 and 1974 there were no turbulences Germany did not experience. And this tempestuous team was only a possibility because Overath knew the route.

CRUYFF: THE VISIONARY

The immoderate nation that reclaimed land from the sea produced a player so unusual he came to be known as "total." Football depends on having players that specialize in certain positions, but with Ajax and with the Clockwork Orange, Johan Cruyff found a way of being everywhere. Rinus Michels's way of operating, with players constantly rotating into one another's positions, needed them to be good on the ball, *and* good at marking, *and* good at shooting.

Cruyff enacted the omnipresence of "total football" to a tee but acted bizarrely everywhere else, eating a sandwich in the dressing room before a match and smoking a cigarette at halftime. He was the first symbolic 10 in that he didn't wear the number on his back, and brought the habits of the team leader into the modern era, on and off the pitch. His shoulder-length hair suited him wonderfully, he was a proponent of sexual liberation when the team traveled together to hotels, and he discovered that the shortest route between two points is a zigzag. Not that he twisted and turned like Pelé, but he ran in short, varying bursts while still keeping hold of the ball.

A three-time Ballon d'Or winner, a World Cup runner-up in 1974, he's widely considered the greatest European player of all time.

Plenty of his statements as manager of Barcelona showed that his thoughts didn't move in entirely straightforward ways either: "If you have the ball you don't need to defend, because there's only one ball"; "If you're winning 4–0 the best thing you can do is hit the post, as that will make the crowd gasp"; "In Spain, players are always rushing around; if there was any point in this, games would only ever end as draws."

When a young Jorge Valdano began arguing with him during a match, Cruyff informed him that he had to address him in the formal *"usted"* form in Spanish, as one does with superiors.

It was only the ball he would let be familiar.

PLATINI: THE ARCHITECT

Like Cruyff, Michel Platini was awarded the Ballon d'Or three times. Convinced he needed to become more versatile as a player, he at one point had a wall built at the height of a defender so that he could work to perfect his deadly free kicks.

At once elegant and rangy, it was very rare for him to miss when he had a shot at goal or a penalty. He was the Serie A top scorer with Juventus, no easy achievement bearing in mind that beating defenders in Italy is as hard as missing siesta.

He'd take up different positions from game to game. When the opposition had good wingers, he'd drop deep to spray forty-yard through balls, thereby bypassing their midfield. When his team was under unbearable pressure, he'd go and play as a second center forward, from which position he'd score headed goals. Like an architect, he'd study the different terrains so he could tell the best way to build an attack.

His intelligence and charisma made him the leader of the France sides of the 1980s. A lover of practical solutions, he performed simple miracles. He called a hat trick he scored in the European Cup "simple": "I just scored one with my left foot, one with my right, and the other with my head."

His repartee was as quick as his passing game. A fan once caught him smoking in a café in Turin—the man was shocked to learn that a top athlete should choose this form of relaxation, and spoke his mind. With notable savoir faire, the Frenchman answered, "As long as Bonini doesn't pick up the habit, we'll be alright." He was referring to Massimo Bonini, who, known as the Marathon Runner, covered the whole pitch in his constant drive to win the ball back.

He never tried out things that he didn't know he could do. His great strength was in his ability to avoid mistakes. Shrewd rather than passionate, he managed to make the most of what he had. No wonder that he became the game's greatest politician in his retirement.

MARADONA: THE REBEL

Never has a player made such a difference to his team, or been so different from everyone else, as Diego Armando Maradona. Villa Fiorito, the shanty-barrio where he was raised and that he bore in his heart, made him play like an extraterrestrial.

Scorer of the greatest legal goal and the greatest illegal goal in the history of the World Cup (both at Mexico '86, both against England), he also led a forgotten club (Napoli) to the scudetto. Arrogant and melodramatic off the pitch, on it he dashed around like a slave trying to save his people. Never has there been such an emotional number 10, nor one to have cried in public to such effect.

His ability to fox his opponents extended to making certain statements that made his myth all the more resounding: "The ball is never dirty"; "It was the hand of God"; "They cut my legs off."

A ninety-minute rebel, he had Che Guevara tattooed on his body, took on FIFA, talked of God as though he were on his team (he pictured Him inhabiting a kind of heavenly dressing room and referred to Him as "Beardy"), and time and again held his hands up to his misdemeanors.

If the result of any World Cup has ever been entirely contingent on a single person, it was Mexico '86. Brazil could have won Mexico '70 without Pelé, who was never team captain and never the main penalty taker. Only Maradona had the ability to drag his team to the summit single-handed.

He was famously kicked about by defenders, but he was hardly a martyr. For him risk is second nature. He's done everything possible to put an end to himself, but without success.

The risks he took as a player would always be resolved by the vast range of answers his left foot could provide. Things were different away from the pitch.

He has flirted with disaster on every possible front. Being the host on a mega-circus of a TV show and leading the Argentine national team are just as fraught with danger as his dalliances with drugs and calorific food, but ultimately his metabolism managed to deal with it all.

So frequent were his improbable feats with the ball—or with a mandarin at parties—that we got to a point of thinking it made sense. But it didn't.

To be number 10 is to be a "Maradona": Hagi was known as the "Maradona of the Carpathians" and Valderrama "El Pibe," or "The Kid."

In the end there's only one "MaraD10S," or "MaraGOD."

BAGGIO: THE FANTASIST

Italy loves a risk-free style of play, and thinks only one player in eleven has any right to an imagination. Like the Pope, the "fantasist" has no equal.

At Mexico '70, Gianni Rivera would play the first half and Sandro Mazzola the other; they couldn't play in the same eleven for fear of sinning by creativity.

From Giuseppe Meazza to Andrea Pirlo, Italy has needed its Leonardo da Vincis to invent the superlative. The most colorful of all was Roberto Baggio, a player who loved to go on mazy runs and was only satisfied if he beat an entire defense, took it around the onrushing keeper, and then finished it, disdainfully, with his weaker foot.

He had such an accurate shot that he once managed a feat that was both pointless and unforgettable. The story goes that someone once covered a ball in paint in a training session and asked Baggio to shoot at distance. With implacable skill, "Il Divino" set about daubing the crossbar.

A Ballon d'Or winner in 1993 and runner-up in the 1994 World Cup, he dazzled in several different strips—proof that his talent could flourish anywhere because it didn't exist within the normal parameters.

What does this tell us about the place of the individual in the Italian game? The "fantasist" is not the apostate who has abandoned his flock; he's just the only one with the authority to do magic. He's not dissimilar to the priest, who may speak with God before anyone else.

With his last touch of the ball at USA '94, he missed an incredibly important penalty. Four years later, in his first match at France '98, he scored one, and showed the kind of presence of mind of a player who had never missed in his life.

A convert to Buddhism, he slalomed between lunging players with such poise that he showed that attacking can also be a form of meditation.

ZINEDINE ZIDANE: THE MYSTIC

With his head shaved like a Zen monk, and the body of a gladiator, Zinedine Zidane's great lesson was that all moves on a football pitch involve the head.

His extreme focus allowed him to score a golden penalty in a European Championships semifinal, two decisive goals in the final of France '98, a stunning volley in the Champions League Final, and a floated "Panenka" penalty in the final at Germany '06.

He was part of the most successful France team in history (World Cup winners and runners-up), and took both Juventus and Real Madrid to the summit of European club football.

Always battling against his own nerves, he also showed how to lose your head. He was rightly sent off in the World Cup by the Mexican referee Arturo Brizio, and his final act as a player was the famous head-butt of Materazzi, after the Italian insulted his family's honor.

Most players try to emulate the gods of Olympus. In the 2006 final in Berlin, Zidane was bidding farewell to the game;

everything he did already had testimonial status. But his final shot wasn't at glory; it returned him to the common mud of his fellow man.

All the greats have tried to be Achilles. Very few have sought to be Hector. Zizou accepted the sentence of being human.

Introverted, heartfelt, and with an intense gaze, he showed that all players have an interior life. His was a mysticism with no need for theology, belonging rather to the human lot.

MESSI: THE GENIUS

Even giants start small. And some are so special that they save themselves the bother of getting any bigger, and yet make clear their exceptional stature. At all of five foot seven, Lionel Messi far exceeds everyone.

In terms of record breaking, he'll be the all-time 10. Four times a Ballon d'Or winner, he's won everything there is to win at club level and is Barcelona's all-time top goal scorer.

Possessed of incredible balance, he tears defenses apart and is prodigiously effective in front of goal, sometimes even scoring after he's been knocked to the ground.

He doesn't go looking for free kicks. He maintains the same burning ambition of a debutant. His obsessive *jouissance* is that of a child or of someone far along the autistic spectrum. And of genius.

Heroism doesn't work a nine to five; it requires epic moments. When it comes to the Battle of Thermopylae, or a World Cup, you have to perform. The only thing left on Messi's to-do list is victory of some kind with the senior Argentina side. (He won the World Cup with the Under-20s in 2005.)

At the time of writing, he's yet to lift the definitive trophy, but one thing he has shown is that a size-small T-shirt can fit a giant.

DIEGO ARMANDO MARADONA: LIFE, DEATH, RESURRECTION, AND A LITTLE MORE BESIDES

THE OPINIONS OF A LEFT FOOTER

On Sunday, October 8, 2000, S.S.C. Napoli retired the number 10 jersey indefinitely. Just another episode in the opera staged by Diego Armando Maradona beside the slopes of Mount Vesuvius. When the god of small feet joined the team in 1984, Napoli had just escaped relegation by a single point. The club enjoyed a fanatical following, but had little to recommend it from a sporting perspective. The Argentine's fifteen-minute presentation as the new signing of Napoli, held at the Stadio San Paolo, was attended by eighty thousand of the devout, and saw him succumb to his second favorite thing to do in public: weeping inconsolably. In truth, the redeemer wasn't in any better state than the team. He'd had a long-term bout of hepatitis, was still recovering from a Goikoetxea-class leg break as well as the disaster of Spain '82, not to mention lengthy disputes with the

Barcelona board of directors and a recently acquired taste for cocaine. At twenty-three years of age, early retirement looked like a distinct possibility.

In the midst of a media free-for-all, receiving injections from unscrupulous doctors, traveling tens of thousands of miles to feature in a friendly, Maradona had been playing matches at a pace of four per week.

Maradona, born in the Eva Perón Hospital, in 1984 upheld his capacity for melodrama and myth making. Napoli was the only Pompeii open to him, an opulent cemetery with sea views. But the precariousness of sky-blue Napoli provided him with the fuel—enthusiasm and resentment—to create a "lowly team to take on the world" and complete the greatest task of any sporting Hercules: the against-all-odds comeback.

In the first match he played in northern Italy, Maradona had his first taste of the racism meted out to Neapolitans. There was a banner that said, "Welcome to Italy: now wash your feet." The child of Villa Fiorito had wound up in the heartland of the poor Italians who decades earlier had sought refuge in the slums of Argentina. In addition to his left boot, he decided to offer up his sentimentalism *cum laude* to Saint Gennaro, patron saint of the city. The results defied all logic: the team that was viewed from the lofty climes of the Milan dressing room as an African horde began winning matches.

Among other wonders, football is full of physical absurdity. Maradona is all of five foot five. During his career as a player he would sleep until 11:00 a.m., had little enthusiasm for jogging, and ate with dead calm (the extra helping of spaghetti on Saturday made its presence felt come the match on Sunday). But his body had a rare tension to it. He could have been wearing a frock coat, and he would still have looked like he was about to murder the ball with a thrust of his chest. He was the greatest and most impulsive artist ever to grace the game, the most dramatic and the most influential within a team. Not even Pelé's leadership was so unanimous. In the 1986 World Cup, Diego managed to convince us that any team with him up front would have been champions. At the European Championships in 2000, Platini compared the Argentine number 10 with football's latest monarch: "Zidane does with a ball what Diego would do with an orange."

Maradona led Napoli to their first scudetto in sixty years, in a division that was formidably rough, and accepted the role of the twentieth century's most publicly kicked man. His turn in the Roman circus was witnessed by a global audience. In came the legions, some from the murky western European steppes, some from the sun-struck plains of the leopard, all of them looking to break his ankles. The Argentine artificer played as his peculiar psychology dictated: with an elemental urgency, like Rookie of the Year out to lock down his place in the team. When he didn't have the ball, he felt more alone than Adam on Mother's Day. He never ceased being the teenager whose tie Menotti had to do up when he was awarded Best Player at the 1979 Youth World Cup in Tokyo.

Napoli gave itself up willingly to this foreign savior. The *bel canto* adopted arias in his honor, every *tavola calda* began including a "Maradona Pizza" on the menu, and the names of various dignitaries were erased from the sidewalks in superfluous honor of the new hero: Via Maradona leading onto Piazza Maradona. Then Argentina knocked Italy out of the 1990 World Cup—in the Stadio San Paolo, no less. The drama was a little too much for the writers at *Gazzette dello Sport*, and a new libretto by Puccini seemed in order: the Spartacus of the South taking on the hosts of imperial Rome. The opera went to penalties. In Neapolitan eyes, Argentina was a more authentic Italy. Their hearts divided, they supported their national side until Maradona's turn came. As the left-footed maestro prepared to take his kick, the Neapolitans couldn't whistle at him, and they bore the outrage in silence when the ball rolled past the keeper—slow, perfect, unreachable. And then they applauded, tears in their eyes, in a state of outright emotional suicide. Never did any of the gladiators win over the enemy in such a way.

THEY SAY I'LL TALK ABOUT ANYTHING, AND THEY'RE RIGHT

On October 8, 2000, Napoli's number 10 jersey became a kind of absence and Maradona wept by satellite, reinforcing his status as a ruined god. His exceptional memoir was in the shops at the time. Its title, *Yo soy el Diego (...de la gente)* (literally, "I Am the People's Diego"), is suggestive of a cloying populism that would put the weepy actress Libertad Lamarque to shame. It cost the publishers a million dollars, making Maradona the best-paid Argentine author never to pen a single book. The first-person account was the work of two journalists who had cut their teeth pitchside, Daniel Arcucci and Ernesto Cherquis Bialo. They were responsible for the book's essential achievement—recreating the authentic and unbridled voice that the maestro was unable to put into writing himself. Unsurprisingly, the book is an unbridled torrent of vanity and narcissism. In an attention-getting business, Diego never hid his vanity—for example when he baptized his own hand, the one he used to score against England, "the hand of God." The crucial thing here is that the expedition of a colossal ego comes accompanied by a frankness that shows the vulnerabilities of, and often aggravates, the author.

For Maradona, teardrops are like punctuation marks, and weeping disconsolately is a way to break up chapters. He sees his life like a tango lyric and has no qualms about taking the blame. Speaking of all the cars he was given as gifts, he describes a classic Mercedes as an affront—he was disappointed at the stick shift. His showiness and bad taste would be worthy of adorning a Vegas casino. Nonetheless, even a person of the most Franciscan austerity would struggle not to be moved by Diego's boyish enthusiasm when he received a present from his wife, a pair of Versace swimming trunks that would be the envy of the most rococo of drug traffickers. Incapable of arguing in a straight line, he draws ingenuously nonsensical conclusions: "I'd rather be a drug addict than a bad friend," he says, as though the only place affections can thrive is inside a cartel.

Vanquished by his own fame, addicted to the press that misunderstands him, the footballer in the confessional of *Yo soy el Diego* sees his tantrums as a form of insurrection. And these outbursts are almost always of the kind you'd expect from

TV-hurling rock stars. The same directors Maradona is at one point ingratiating himself with, he earlier on reviled; he lambasts the national team's lack of "dignity" and goes off shark fishing but rejoins the camp after a few days; he arraigns teammates who try to control the team, while applauding the executives at Napoli who bought players on his recommendation. When he's in the right, the scope is pretty limited: João Havelange, a water poloist turned politician, doesn't deserve his place in the game; FIFA shouldn't permit eleven men suffering from diarrhea to play at midday in Mexico, at an altitude of seven thousand feet, and at "ravioli time." Maradona is quite right to stand up for oft-abused players, but it's a rather grand mistake for him to model himself as a liberator, a Túpac Amaru in shorts.

His impulsive statements have for years been given a disproportionately large media forum. Jorge Valdano summed it up better than anyone: the way he's listened to, it's as though Maradona also opines with his left foot. In 2002, "The Fuzz" announced his intention to have his own TV show, "like David Letterman." Having dictated on the pitch, he wanted to dispense his left-footed opinions off it, too.

Maradona could never be suspected of being consistent, but his confessions in Yo soy el Diego come across like a sustained torrent of passion. By comparison, how watered down seems Jimmy Burns's far more serious and well-documented report, The Hand of God, as it rummages around in its protagonist's dirty washing, makes connections between him and the Neapolitan Mafia, and him and the everlasting legs of the model Heather Parisi, goes in search of illegitimate children, and explores the harrowing addictions of Napoli's very own king of the snort. Inevitably, Burns leaves numerous strands untied, but this isn't what makes his thorough examination inferior to the fragmentary breaches of trust contained in *Yo soy el Diego*; it's because it lacks Maradona's precise tone as he faces his failures. It's difficult to imagine other decorated sporting figures writing with honesty about their spectacular errors, let alone all the awful bastards they hate.

But the mind of the boy from Villa Fiorito is never one-dimensional. The magnificent recriminations, which so humanize him, contrast with his poor imitations of the "footballer with a conscience," à la Eric Cantona. He places excessive emphasis on trying to make his struggle to survive seem political. His civic idols are a mishmash of Fidel Castro, Carlos Saúl Menem, and the Che Guevara tattooed on his arm. In 2001 he allowed himself to be interviewed at length, by the Italian Gianni Mina, for the first time since his medical withdrawal in Cuba. In a mixture of Spanish and Italian weighed down by the isolation and the medication, he compared Celia Cruz with an orangutan for having opposed the government of the island and claimed that the history of Latin America had not been accurately told. The latter insight came to him on a private-jet ride over the Andes, when he realized there was no way San Martín could have crossed them on foot, as the legend had it. The man who needs to hire an airplane in order to disagree with received history isn't going to be accepted into the ranks of the Left all that readily, and yet there is always something rebellious to Diego, a touch of anarchism that sets him apart from the divas and brings him closer to the people. "The Fuzz" is one of the Guevarist tribe. Place him inside a luxury chalet and he'll give the place a touch of an encampment.

Perhaps out of envy for the players, the FIFA executives never miss a chance to stick the boot in. At the close of the twentieth century they carried out a survey on the best player of the era, an undertaking as harebrained as the UN proposing a hit parade of their favorite countries. The experts chose Pelé; the Internet went for Maradona. Diego delighted in the result: the ground troops had chosen him against the generals' wishes. Edson Arantes came out of it looking like a docile idol, manipulated by the system, unable to make himself heard.

Though Pelé's stats are better, no player has ever had such complete command over a team as Maradona. His rule was absolute, particularly in groups that were up against it, and in no-hoper squads (whether it was Napoli or Bilardo's unpopular Argentina side). When the winds favored him, he wasn't so good. When victory seemed guaranteed (at Barcelona, or at Spain '82 when Argentina were defending champions), he tripped at the hurdles. Paranoia and mistrust were the ingredients for his victories. At the '86 World Cup, the trainer Carlos Salvador Bilardo acted like his own private Iago, whispering intrigues in his ear that forced him into a furious creativity.

Maradona bore the mark of the beast. He only needed the ball to be given to him on the halfway line to have a chance of winning a match. This power, perhaps, took a peculiar toll psychologically. So just as left wingers have a tendency to live on the margins, and as goalkeepers get used to making decisions for themselves and having rules that apply to them alone, the total leader does not entertain the thought of a problem that he can't feint his way past. Diego created a world in the image of his desires, so superabundant that reality—the magic-less mist that encircles life outside the stadium—itself was evaded.

In his battle against the other great number 10, Maradona has been fond of quoting Rivellino, the legendary winger who kidded Pelé about wishing he had been left-footed. For the lovers of capriciousness, the virtuosity of the left foot is a fundamental principle.

Is there one particular scene that can possibly summarize the turbulent career of the gladiator with the butcher's body? If I had to pick one, I'd go for the moment he roared into the camera at USA '94. It was Diego's return to the World Cup after the turmoil of Italia '90, the cocaine "raviolis" he was found with in Buenos Aires, the numerous testaments that here was a boy with the dirt of Villa Fiorito still stuck to his feet. His most important moves had begun happening off the pitch, and his body had begun announcing his retirement for him. Nonetheless, in the match against Greece he took the ball as he would have done in the days when he would shoot for fun, and planted it in the corner of the goal. He would later be pulled aside for a drug test (which may not have been random), and ephedrine would be found in his system, a drug that gives the lungs a boost but that would also make it harder to shoot with any accuracy. We saw him leave the field smiling, a blonde female nurse at his side. The Argentine writer Juan Sasturain called to mind a terrible adage of Raymond Chandler's from *The Long Goodbye*: "All blondes have their points." That day, as the sun in Boston beat down, it was a happy Maradona the nurse led to the gallows.

His downfall thereafter was definitive, and all that was left to him was the compensatory posterity of scandal: the crazy statements, rehab, a car crash in Cuba, his terrible appearance no one could tear their eyes away from—a fat man with orange hair and piercings under his armpits.

But let's pause his legend at that last, incredible goal. Having beaten the keeper, Diego wheeled away to celebrate, suddenly spotted a camera, ran over to it. and roared into the lens—like some wounded beast. The untouchable, the lion, in the eyes of FIFA, was back in his kingdom. The victim of so much admiration was out for revenge.

He never got it.

DYING TO CONVINCE

In 2004, the Colombian magazine Soho *set itself the task of predicting when certain famous people would die. All of us who have worked in journalism know what an unwelcome task it is to write obituaries, a job that has to be done ahead of the fact.*

When I worked at La Jornada Semanal *we had a box we called "the cooler"—into it went the names of those whose imminent deaths, their lives having been so very noteworthy, would come as no surprise. At a newspaper, few things are likely to show you up quite as much as an inability to explain who the dead person was. Though thankless, this speculative task is an essential part of making sure the news is*

*on time. It was in the job of predicting deaths that Antonio Tabucchi
found the melancholy traits he needed for the protagonist in* Pereira
Maintains.

I accepted the job from Soho *because it meant the chance to
give an account of Maradona's supremacy once and for all, without
him having to die to convince me. I would make the most of the
imaginary drama of his disappearance so as to avoid endless reruns
of the debate as to the relative merits of Alfredo Di Stéfano, Pelé,
and Maradona, which, really, is like comparing pears, apples, and
watermelons.*

*If Onetti discovered that a single person is capable of living various
brief lives, Maradona found he had been given the ability to
overcome various brief deaths. In this momentary eclipse, a man in
fact destined for the vagaries of survival is captured in the amber of
a fictional obituary.*

Three pieces of news have changed the course of the planet: the
privatization of the Great Wall of China, the earthquake that
laid low Mexico City, and the death of Diego Armando
Maradona. I write these lines with the full guilt and pain of the
survivor. The single edifice visible from the moon has become a
theme park, the city where I was born is now a labyrinth where
stray dogs roam, and the greatest football player of all time has
kicked his last ever ball.

Maradona's greatness was testified by the decisions of football
leagues around the world to suspend all matches for the course of
a Sunday. A strange posthumous consensus has followed the left
footer's death. For fans of Boca Juniors, the "Fuzzy One" was

a deity with the number 10 on his back. Several sentimental songs and the fervor of the hooligans made it thus, but no one seriously thought it was possible for such a contentious figure to become a figurehead for the whole tribe.

We've heard Franz Beckenbauer, leaving a lunch with the FIFA president, say for the first time that he never saw another player like Maradona; Johan Cruyff said the same following a golf match. A number of Argentine players plying their trade in the Mexican leagues proposed a charity match in aid of the earthquake victims, as well as the idea of building a "Maradona Housing Unit" in the heart of the devastated city. And word came from China: a black band would be placed on the Great Wall to mark the passing of the Argentine maestro.

Truly, no one expected the consensus to form so quickly on a subject as divisive as football. The fans' global memory and, consequently, the desire to discuss and debate, came about with the advent of television. The old reels do little justice to certain titans. We know that Di Stéfano was the "Blond Arrow" and that he would kiss the ball at the end of every match. The Catalans, whom history has endowed with a prodigious memory for tragedies, recall the fact the player, having been bound for Barca, after the intervention of the government of the day ended up at Real Madrid. Whatever the case, when he left Argentina for Spain, Di Stéfano went on to become the immutable emblem of the Merengues, whom he still supports to this day from the box seats. We accept his legend in the same way we accept those old, vaguely great surnames that were used to christen ocean currents, gin cocktails, or luxury automobiles.

Modern football needed another king, someone made global by TV. Pelé was the greatest of his day, and was universally visible. His record has never been surpassed: three World Cups, the first at the age of sixteen. Once he'd been named "The King," he assumed, like any monarch, that he'd never abdicate or be substituted by another.

As an idol that aspired to become an institution, Edson Arantes knew how to play the game outside the pitch, too. When he heard that Maradona had died, he is quoted as having said "He was better than me"—words in which most commentators discerned greatness, a gesture that confirmed Pelé's deserved possession of the scepter. One even recounted, echoing Ortega y Gasset, that the definition of aristocracy is the renunciation of rights and the will to devolve duties, and that it took a king such as Pelé to show such generosity to a commoner.

Edson Arantes is no stranger to politics. As Minister for Sport, he introduced the Pelé Law, freeing players to sign to whichever club they chose, even in their teens. This measure put free will in alignment with the market economy—a good reflection of King Pelé's own character.

In a sport with people given to unaccountable tastes and moods, Pelé's eccentricities amounted to little more than an obsessive liking for blondes, or stunts such as turning up at the 1974 World Cup in Germany dressed in red, white, and blue, the colors of his sponsor, Pepsi. The cadence of his life is not an easy one to whistle along to. The boy who played at night on the sand, with the moon his only witness, went on to be adopted by Santos and later by the national team. Among the many moves he invented during his reign, none was as good as his celebration: an elastic somersault and twist, proof that there's nothing so elegant as triumph.

The Brazilian was so widely admired that his thousandth goal had a TV audience like that for Armstrong's lunar landing. Even his stint in the MLS was a prime-time event. He played for the Cosmos alongside another deluxe pre-retiree, Franz Beckenbauer. And when the tricky moment came to say goodbye, he executed it without losing the samba rhythm that is his very biography. He visited the poor barrios, his arms full of toys, he played beach football with the children, he lent his weight to UNICEF. In his TV commentary work he reinforced his aura of an excessively good-intentioned icon: he only saw good players.

The death of the Argentine number 10 has prompted revisions to the hagiography. Like Pelé, Maradona rose out of a miserable barrio and made it to the very top: Youth World Cup Champion in 1979, World Champion in 1986, finalist in 1990. But his was a flickering brilliance. That Menotti didn't pick him for Argentina in '78 prevented him from claiming an early crown; he came to Spain '82 as the great Argentine hope and part of the best eleven in the country's history, but failed, partly because of the quality of the competition (Brazil and Italy) and partly because of the mood among those representing a country then at war in the Falklands. His last World Cup was problematic, too: for his farewell, he was led away by the anti-doping nurse, an innocent smile etched on his face. He tested positive for a strong cold medicine, which no one could overly blame him for, but which also left an irreparable dent in his reputation.

Private vice becomes all the more mouthwatering in a world where ill deeds, seen by hidden eyes, always sell. Maradona was the author of insane goals, but certain sections of the press prefer the photos of him dressed as a woman at a party with Careca, or with a somewhat shinier smile than that of someone who only had cereal for breakfast. Because the concept of limits was foreign to him, this prima donna was also a sitting duck. Every match he played, he played with the enthusiasm of the debutant, and there weren't any pleasures he enjoyed "just a bit." When he arrived in Napoli in 1984 and tried the *spaghetti aglio, olio e pepperoncino*, it was clear that he was going to put on weight with the assistance of this impossible-to-refuse delicacy. He had contracted the most dangerous of his addictions not long before. He'd found Barcelona cold and demanding, and taken consolation in a product widely consumed in the region that would later on have a song named after it by Estopa: cocaine. Someone who knows the ball exists for him to kick hundreds of times without it touching the ground was never going to be less than liberal with the white stuff.

The greatest psychological challenge for footballers is the distance separating the pitch from the rest of the world. They say the privatization of the Great Wall made Maradona extremely angry. What he lacked was dikes, ways of separating one environment from another.

On the island of the pitch, Diego showed exemplary humility; away from it, he exploded like a dramatic supernova. Never has a sporting icon sworn so much on his daughters' names. A histrionic figure, he found his ideal theater in Napoli. It wasn't designer-boutique Italy he played for, but the Italy of those fire stokers who found a cheap way of combating hunger in the form of the pizza.

I was at the Stadio San Paolo when Argentina knocked Italy out of the 1990 World Cup, aided by a Maradona penalty kick. After the match I went to eat with an Argentine friend I used to go to games with. He had been away from his homeland for a long time, living in Israel; it's no exaggeration to say he only felt Argentine when he watched football. But then again, he didn't have much fondness for the game in general, which added to the strangeness of his character.

Argentina was a gypsy side at Italia '90. No one expected them to make the final. Each time the *albiceleste* seemed about to go out, my friend booked tickets to the Greek islands, and each time he had to cancel them. He spent half the championship at the travel agency.

Following Argentina's most surprising triumph, the only restaurant we could get into was a Chinese place. Every single diner was a foreigner. The Neapolitans had decided to go home to ponder over despair's discreet lasagna. The festive mood spread around the tables as we shared those sweet wines that are German but can only be found in Chinese restaurants. In the midst of this jubilation, one of these anonymous men who pass their lives preparing the chop suey with no passport or other kind of ID, came out of the kitchen bearing an immense Italian flag, and, in an Esperanto made more comprehensible by his enthusiasm, shouted, "Viva Maradona! Maradona is international!" Why was it the Italian flag he was waving? Because it was the only one he could lay his hands on, surely, and his exaltation required a flag. Furthermore, his international utterance suggested that even Italy ought to have supported someone as international as Maradona. The Argentine 10 drew to him the strangest desires to belong, including those of a Chinese man who worked as a chef, the commonest job for people who don't exist on paper.

As for Argentines, their fondness for Maradona is in no doubt. What's strange is the extremes it reaches, even by unbridled *porteño* standards. "No one has made me as happy in my entire life," a taxi driver in Buenos Aires told me, a serious sufferer of Diego dependence.

Maradona never wanted for affection, and this, in one way, contributed to his downfall. The star distanced himself from formal logic and bowled on into the third act of the opera. The first had been his rise from misery, the second his anguished glories. Then the period of his downfall—the tabloid period. The overweight retiree laid into photographers, made strident political statements, came out of detox, and checked into the house of the overdose. Perhaps this public immolation was for him a desperate way to prolong the same sacrificial fury that had carried him to the summit.

His retirement resembled that of O. J. Simpson, the man who learned to run from poverty and transformed his paranoia into the art of the escape. Simpson devoured record yards for the Buffalo Bills, and after retiring appeared in TV ads running to catch a plane. Something in his blood made him keep on running. His wife was stabbed and he escaped in a Ford Bronco.

The cameras followed him—as they had done inside the stadiums—until finally he gave himself up. His Houdini capabilities didn't stop when he went to court. The assassin's glove looked like a great fit, but the idol escaped justice.

Maradona's last resort was both more sincere and more tragic. When FIFA pulled him out of the World Cup, he said, "They've chopped my legs off." The hero died a little at a time. When he withdrew to Cuba, like Jensen's *Gradiva*, he was able to say, "I have long grown used to being dead." Incapable of embracing football's obvious posterities (commentator, manager, director), even the subdued form of the sporting beyond—opening an Argentine restaurant—held no appeal.

Diego's demolition of his own reputation had in it something of a rare, pure gesture. In the end, only his actions on the pitch were praiseworthy. Is there not something bordering on the religious in this essentialism? Maradona squandered that which the world gave him so that the only thing left was the reason they gave it to him.

There's only been one king in football, Pelé, but there's only been one slave-cum-liberator in the history of the sport as well. The Villa Fiorito-leaver was far from being nobility. He was as fueled by insults as he was by the misery of his beginnings. In what is a team game, his individual qualities reached a higher limit: that magic moment when the ten men playing alongside him believed they were also exceptional.

A loss can sometimes have the effect of revealing something that was always there but could only become powerful in its absence. There are moments in the world when certain givens are reconsidered. The Mexico earthquake could have killed more people, and it is also possible that the privatization of the Great Wall and its new neon decorations could have been avoided. It is only by opening wounds that lessons can be taken from them.

Diego Armando Maradona is dead. Only once in football has a single man been all men.

THE NIGHT DIEGO SAVED MARADONA

Just when no one was expecting it, Maradona turned to a favorite recourse of the gods: resurrection. In 2004 he had begun to resemble a sumo wrestler, his gaze had become erratic, and he had been making statements that, while indubitably candid, often had very little to do with reality.

On August 15, 2005, emanating the same implacable authority as in his playing days, the idol who had tried everything he could to destroy himself made an appearance in the greatest sanctuary mass culture has to offer: TV. The first surprise was how good he looked physically; he'd never been blessed with the most Olympic of metabolisms. Diego had merely to catch a whiff of a plate of macaroni to start putting on weight, but following a tummy tuck in a Colombian clinic in Cartagena de Indias, he was flaunting it like in his days captaining the national side.

Even so, the most striking thing wasn't his slimness, but that his eyes had regained the capacity to focus again, with all the precision of someone scanning for the top corner of the net. So deep were his levels of concentration when *La noche del 10* first went to air that he managed not to cry—a feat in itself.

The set had been custom built to fit his passions: a mix of samba parade ground, beach-football pitch, sports-car fair, beauty contest, and musical comedy. No stranger to immoderation, the Argentine number 10 was a natural when it came to steering a series of excesses. The defining moment in the first episode was King Pelé's appearance.

History has always had a liking for paradox: the rebel player turning host to the diplomat player. Having shot darts at one another through the years, the two greats met up on *La noche del 10*. Many saw it as the closest thing in football to the meeting between San Martín and Bolívar to decide the leadership of Latin America.

But all historical metaphors were left in the locker room. The encounter was more normal than expected. Among other things, Pelé and Diego showed with great aplomb that they are passionate—and terrible—singers, seeking relief for their problems.

2005 was a difficult year for Pelé. His son had been arrested for links with the drug world. The first thing he said to his old rival was, "You are an example." He was referring not to Diego's goals, which circulate in the mediasphere, but rather the way he had overcome his inner enemy. "This isn't a miracle," said the Fuzzy One with equanimity, while the audience wept to see the miracle.

In addition to hosting *La noche del 10*, in 2005 Diego worked with Emir Kusturica on a biopic of his life. *Loving Maradona*, a documentary by Javier Vázquez, premiered at the end of the year and was an impeccable testimony to the passions inspired by the left footer—from Villa Fiorito, taking in the Church of Maradona, whose headquarters are in Rosario, Argentina, and which has tens of thousands of parishioners, to the Maradona River, thus named by a young group of explorers in the south of Argentina, and the many, many Maradona tattoos.

But it also registers the flip side of Diego dependence: his hounding by the media, his lack of privacy, the vicious urgency that goes into wringing statements from the man when he doesn't want to—and sometimes can't—make them.

The standout part in the film features Maradona when he was at his lowest ebb, as an inflated monster inhabiting a Cuban Xanadu. There are his usual fascinatingly mischievous disclosures ("I wanted to be a doctor when I was growing up—what an imbecile!"), but it's painful viewing. Vázquez shows him here during his deterioration, when his true life exists only in his past, in the fairytale plays he made, in the memories of his childhood friends or the people who so loved him in Napoli.

By a strange sort of symbiosis, the old football player came increasingly to resemble the object on which his fate hinged: the ball. How different from his youthful self, that restless, slightly lost gaze of the archive images. *Loving Maradona* is propelled by the past up until the final scene when the twinkle-toed prima donna appears dancing in a TV studio, wreathed in smoke, apparently floating on some heavenly substance. Following years of destruction, one single appearance gives him back that miraculous air.

As Jacobus de Voragine shows in the collected hagiographies of *The Golden Legend*, the episodes to which faith lends a nimbus are at once surprising and logical. The Church of Maradona was disposed to wait for an annihilator-martyr, or for an unprecedented rescue. From adolescence onwards, everything has been possible when it comes to Diego.

One of Maradona's brothers is asked, in *Loving Maradona*, whether he can compare with him. With all the wisdom of childhood, he answers, "My brother's from another planet." The show, with all its flaunting, all the smoke and thunder, is the extraterrestrial's landing platform.

But Argentina's indelible number 10 didn't only come back from the dead on camera: he also became vice president of Boca Juniors, the club closest to his heart.

When he made his debut as a TV presenter in August 2005, it was confirmation of the stuff of which popular heroes are made, and the importance of the return in people's imagination. As Samuel Beckett, who was crazy about football, said: "There is no return leg between a man and his destiny." The period Maradona spent ruining himself was sufficient to show the validity of the pronouncement. At Spain '82, Gentile kicked Maradona mercilessly, showing just how ironic the names of gladiators can be. The setback Diego suffered during his retirement years was even harsher, as though destiny were under the orders of Helenio Herrera. But when reality began corralling him in the direction of death or ridicule, what came back to the Argentina captain was that sense of "us against the world."

Beckett's prophecies were rarely wrong. One evening, in a rainy field, misfortune donned its gloves. There is no second leg. Diego submitted himself to the sentence, accepting it between tears and self-accusations as harsh as those of a Rousseau or a Saint Augustine, but in fewer words: "I fucked it." When fate was grazing his ankles, he came up with a jink, finding a most wondrous vanishing point. The maestro who gave half a dozen Englishmen the slip in the Estadio Azteca now, for once, managed to evade himself.

Diego refers to his drug spree in the following way: "When I was dead." Having his own TV show is the closest thing the global village has to offer in terms of a return from the afterlife. The decadence of Elvis, in many ways similar to that of Diego, led to his grotesque end and gave rise to the compensatory rumors about the King of Rock 'n' Roll living on in ghostly form. Maradona managed the same thing without going through the discomfort of actually dying. He returned from the place of no return.

Just as Diego's tastes are Taj Mahal-like in scale, the sensibility of his show had to be overelaborate. The number 10 cut off the orchestra to sing a tango about a wretched boy who dreamed of being him: "Mama, mama, I'll get money, I'll be a Maradona, a Batistuta, a Pelé." Diego's latest incarnation wanted to be Diego! The great sentimental display of his return brought him back to the beginning, and in this fairytale beginning he recovered the primitive innocence. A child once more, he asked for Pelé's autograph. Then he invited him to play keepy-uppy.

For an Earthling who doesn't care about the uproar inside stadiums, it could be that two middle-aged men heading a ball back and forth doesn't mean much. For a pitchside devotee, it constitutes a strange mirage. As the ball passed from Diego's forehead to Pelé's, it seemed a kind of verification of football's fragile prodigies, its contagious madness. What does it matter that two men prevent a ball inflated with air from dropping to the ground? In the world's inventory, there is only one object that can be put in orbit with the head. As the earth turned on its axis, Pelé and Maradona kept up their part in the scale of things.

If Achilles had read the *Iliad* and gone around blowing his own trumpet, that would have been insufferable: "Sing, muse, the wrath of Achilles..." Maradona is a stranger to modesty and has a tendency to refer to God as though He were his press spokesperson. But he made a mess of things for such a long while and his own torments were so public that he has become another person in order to recount his story.

Regarding Maradona, Vázquez Montalbán asked himself, "If he had been one of the Olympian gods, what other role might he have aspired to?" TV, with its capacity to make his ghosts appear as if "live," provided a singular rite of passage: Maradona as spectator to himself. The idol immersed in the mania of fame finally placed himself in the position of his fans.

The hero was saved by the child.

GOD COMMITTING SUICIDE?

In 2008, Diego Armando Maradona made the reckless decision to manage the Argentine national side. A country held its breath at the potential ruination of its favorite son.

Called into question by its intoxications, football needs the tonic of Maradona to wake up. Unlike most of his teammates, the one-time *albiceleste* captain has never ceased seeking out challenges, or problems. It isn't by chance that in 2010 an insurance company signed him up to advertise himself as someone who lives in a state of risk while others pray for his safety.

Blessed with exceptional physical resistance, Maradona survived his diet of excesses. His addictive temperament led him to consider numerous ways of exiting the stage. All of them led to unexpected ways back onto the stage.

I visited the offices of Argentine newspaper *La Nación* in November 2008 to meet Daniel Arcucci, coauthor of *Yo soy el Diego*. According to Arcucci, after years of the kinds of ups and downs one associates with an electrocardiogram, the left footer's fate is as follows: "Diego moves in cycles. When it seems like he's done for, he comes back out on top. It's always been the way. He first announced he'd had enough of football in 1977! Diego's often had enough. What's happened is that the cycles have grown shorter. Before, years would pass between the successes and the failures, now it's every other day."

The essence of a superhero is his bipolarity—breakfasting on Clark Kent's bland cereal and at dinnertime avoiding the Kryptonite that Superman cannot metabolize. Maradona's bipolarity has been an extreme case; the thrall in which he holds people is due in great part to his condition as self-destructive victor. According to Arcucci, the years have seen an intensification of the ups and downs. Away from the rigors of the training pitch, it became a matter of will if he was going to avoid the temptations of a society that promises instant gratification to anyone with enough cash in the bank.

With a little under two years to go before the World Cup in South Africa, Diego had sufficient time to awaken dreams that weren't very durable. He made Bilardo his number two, injecting a little realism into the fantastical tale.

In November 2008, upon hearing the news that Maradona would lead the national team, most Argentines were skeptical. The player's managerial inexperience worried them less than the damage the idol might do to himself. It was like the statue of San Martín had suddenly set off toward a battle he looked likely to lose.

The God decided to play with fire. When referring to his colleague up on high, he calls him "Beardy" or "the *real* God." A prisoner in the circus of idolatry, he has gone to almost impossible lengths to make the mistakes that would prove him to be human. The strange thing is that he has failed.

With no other credential but his passion for the game that he, among others, had reinvented, Maradona accepted what was on offer: glory or utter ruin. Those who had given him up for dead looked on in 2005 at his self-resurrection in the provisional heaven of television. Just when he seemed to be mellowing as a grandfather, preparing to teach tricks to the baby his daughter had with "Kun" Agüero, the abyss again began tugging at his sleeve.

Like Borges's immortal, Maradona has looked in vain for the river whose waters would confer mortality. The disasters brought him no closer to the common state of his fellow creatures—on the contrary, they showed how indestructible he was. When God fires at himself he shows supernaturally steady hands, but the bullets are all blanks.

The knockout route to South Africa didn't turn out to be his immolation, but it bore a striking resemblance. Bolivia put several goals past Argentina, whose qualification was a last-ditch affair against Uruguay, beneath rains that made the game hard to see. That match saw Diego almost more emotional than ever, and he told the journalists who had doubted him they could "carry on sucking it."

A legend gradually began to form: the Argentina of 2010 had a lot of the 1986 side about it—the side Maradona led to the title. The theme of the double, so important in Argentine culture, was reinforced by the presence of Messi, who in a Spanish league match had already reproduced Diego's goal against England. The parallels became astonishing; in 1986 no one had believed in a team that had an excess of forwards and was reliant on the inspirations of its number 10; the qualifying stages had been mediocre, and it wasn't until the quarterfinals that the best starting eleven was settled on.

If Leo Messi's genius exploded on the pitch, everything would be fine. Maradona came out at the start of South Africa 2010 in a new guise: bearded like an Orthodox Church leader and wearing a gray suit, he clutched a calming rosary. A priest of inscrutable seriousness. No God this time, but rather a transmitter of the faith. Standing pitchside, he tried to make his charisma spread to new messiahs—not to mention Messi himself.

Unfortunately for Maradona, Messi played only very well—inexcusable behavior for a genius. His shots didn't end up being unstoppable. At the end of each match Diego gave in to sentiment, hugging and kissing his players as though yearning to be one of them. These shows of affection were his optimal strategy. Can embraces be used to drill a team? If anyone was capable of such a sentimental miracle, that person was Maradona.

Each time the ball went out of play, and he touched it with his street shoes, the fans went crazy in acknowledgment of the magic contained in Diego's feet.

In a BBC documentary on the Berlin Philharmonic, one of the musicians recounts a rehearsal in which the orchestra began playing as though under the guidance of a magic impulse. What had happened? At that moment the first violin was leading, but a door had opened at the back of the rehearsal space. The silhouette of Furtwängler could be seen in the doorway. The mere presence of a conductor-genius had been a stimulus to the orchestra.

Maradona hoped for similar in South Africa. The main thing he could contribute was just being there. His players were good enough to work out their own tactics. Argentina won their first four matches convincingly. The magnetic effect of God-become-missionary seemed to be doing the trick.

But the usual way in football is that mystical illusions become subject to religious reform—that is, to Germany. Argentina were beaten 4–0 by a young and industrious group of Teutons. The humiliation made clear what people had sensed beforehand: Diego was no tactician. As always, luck and moments of inspiration for the opposition played their parts, but Argentina were also just too weak.

In any case, the World Cup performance hadn't been an out-and-out disaster. Rather, it was neither here not there, which left the manager with a chance of keeping his job. The danger lover's decision? Roll the dice again, of course. But then he was fired. Even so, he didn't rule out returning; you never can with Diego.

RONALDO:
THE WAY OF ALL FLESH

FOR BRAZILIAN PLAYERS, it's harder to make a name on your own than to win the World Cup. Ronaldo Luís Nazário de Lima, also known as The Phenomenon, accomplished the remarkable feat of coming to be known as just "Ronaldo."

He was sixteen when he first joined the national side in 1994. Though too young to play, he traveled with the squad to USA '94, which he watched from the sidelines. There was another Ronaldo in the squad, Ronaldo Rodrigues de Jesus, who was from São Paulo, so the younger of the two was nicknamed "Ronaldinho," or "little Ronald."

He took part in the 1996 Olympics in Atlanta. The city that gave the world Coca-Cola was introduced to the new icon of pop culture who went by the diminutive now printed on his shirt: "Ronaldinho." A year on, no one would dare to call him that. He moved to Holland, joining PSV Eindhoven and scoring forty-two goals in forty-nine matches. He sprinted across the pitches as though reclaiming the Low Country's land from the sea.

From then on, if anyone had the gall to use the same name as him, they had to make adjustments. A certain Ronaldo de Assis Moreira would fish out the diminutive his namesake had thrown in the bin, having a very successful career as "Ronaldinho." And the Portuguese Cristiano Ronaldo dos Santos Aveiro may have been able to take on cyborg-like names, but has never been able to simply call himself Ronaldo.

At thirty-four years of age, the World Cup top scorer (fifteen goals, including two in the 2002 final), a La Liga winner with Real Madrid, a UEFA Cup winner with Barcelona and Inter, and a two-time Ballon d'Or winner (1997 and 2002), made the most interesting statement of his life in the spotlight: "I'm retiring not because of my mind, but because of my body."

It was the first time he'd ever alluded to his psychology. It's possible to see his career as one of immense waste, one in which no amount of mental effort would make his physical being obey.

Along with Roberto Carlos, Ronaldo ushered in a fashion for two things: fearsome shaved heads and unrelenting Brazilians. Unlike his compatriots, who played at a samba pace and would have ad hoc siestas mid-pitch, The Phenomenon was not only precociously talented, but also in a terrible hurry. When he spearheaded an attack he found out what a positive thing solitude can be, becoming highly antisocial, limiting his contact with anything to shots on goal.

Ronaldo's style, which mixed corpulence with sheer skill, was that of a designer gladiator. His height, six feet, meant his weight should have been around 180 pounds, but it's hard to live by the body without succumbing to its temptations, particularly in a world where the spaghetti is so delicious. Ronaldo touched 220 pounds on several occasions, and was still brilliant. For all the graffiti on the rooftops of Rio de Janeiro about his obesity, he settled that by being fat but fast, and smiling like the Buddha of the gymnasiums.

Unlike Figo, who was handsome like a character in an operetta, and who pretended to be passionate about made-up things, Ronaldo was only loyal to his desires. His egoism during a match was dazzling but highly effective; outside of game time, he gave his heart to a wide array of swimwear models and was once photographed at a party with a transvestite on his arm. We already know that love, while it lasts, is eternal. And Ronaldo's eternities were especially swift.

Manuel Vázquez Montalbán described Ronaldo's unique qualities like this: "I'm afraid Ronaldo will pass through life and through history without having understood a thing about what was, and is, really going on. And it isn't as though we can even see him as a high-end immigrant. He is not, and never will be, a club player." He wasn't even loyal to Jairzinho, a World Cup winner with Brazil in 1970, who unearthed his talent as a boy. When Ronaldo was making that end-of-career speech, he forgot to mention his mentor. The great Jair felt affronted; he knew that the bucktoothed player only needed other people so that he could slalom past them on the pitch, but some mention still seemed reasonable. The Phenomenon said goodbye in the same way that he had played—without a clue about the people around him.

In both Italy and Spain he turned out for archenemies, without seeming to be aware of the fact. True, he didn't move directly between Barcelona and Real Madrid, or Inter and AC Milan, but he was quite disconnected from the hopes and dreams of the fans. As snugly as the ball stuck to his foot, he was detached and distant from his environment.

At seventeen he had a lot of Pelé about him. Four years later, at France '98, commentators seemed unable to say his name without adding "the best player in the world" every time. So much was expected from him and the special boots Nike made for him that on the eve of the final he was suffering from extreme nervous tension and had convulsions just before the game. In the country that had promulgated the Rights of Man, The Phenomenon was forced to play like a zombie. He made an effort but left the Stade de France looking lost, the 3–0 defeat barely seeming to have registered. It was a miracle he got away alive.

What's the shelf life on an attacker who leaves defenses uprooted in his thirty-yard wake? Or, how long could he last in Italy, where fouls are haute couture? It was impossible to slalom past so many tattooed legionnaires with "designs" on him. On December 21, 1999, the knee of The Phenomenon was in shreds.

His body handed him the bill, and he soon became a famous young retiree. X-ray scans of his knees were published in the papers, just as photos of his first celebrity girlfriend, Susana Werner or "La Ronaldinha," had once been.

In 2002 it was clear to the football prognosticators that the game depended not on a crystal ball but only on the state of Ronaldo's knee. And he managed the comeback worthy of a hero.

He even allowed himself the luxury of that strange fringe haircut, which made his cranium resemble a tropical fruit, though no one was making fun. Brazil won the next World Cup with him as their figurehead.

And there was still time for an outstanding run in the Real Madrid Galactico side, with whom he won the Champions League in 2002, and he went to the World Cup in 2006 to add to his tally in that tournament. True to the inconstancy he showed throughout his career, he finished his playing days with Corinthians, the local rivals of the team he began his career with, Flamengo.

The ups and downs in his career were due to a dodgy knee, but also his way of combating the tedium, depression, and other occupational hazards of a life overdosed with models. The nightclub was his therapy room.

After it was over with Susana Werner, Ronaldo proposed to another supermodel, Daniella Cicarelli. The wedding took place in the castle at Chantilly, an apt setting for the spur-of-the-moment prince who could never say no to a bowl of ice cream.

An out-and-out goal collector, Ronaldo also hoped to notch up his fair share of ladies who donned bikinis professionally. His contact with girls from other professions didn't end well, among other things because three of them weren't girls, but transvestites who were out to blackmail him.

During the 2002 World Cup, he met a Brazilian waitress in a Tokyo restaurant and ended up having a child with her (not in the restaurant, of course, though that would have been fitting for someone who was always in a rush to move on to the next thing). In 2010 he decided to avoid all possibility of becoming a father again, announcing his vasectomy in a press conference.

Ronaldo's private life has been as public and physically demanding as his chosen profession. As for his interior life, there are some doubts over whether such a thing exists.

On Valentine's Day in 2011, Ronaldo Luís Nazário de Lima summed up his own tragedy like this: he'd realized that his mind was stronger than his body. Had he worked this out at the start of his career, he might have ended up being judged alongside the likes of Di Stéfano, Pelé, Maradona, Cruyff, or Beckenbauer. When he was bearing down on goal, he was the child chasing after an ice-cream truck: there was no way to hold back either his strength or his desire. Like a Triton or a centaur, he belonged to a class of fabular beings. He was The Phenomenon.

Born the same year as Shakira, he resembled a personage from a different era, the antiquity in which he took to the arena like a gladiator. In the media frenzy that is football, he survived in the only way he knew how: by wearing himself down even more. He lost the physical battle, but conquered his name.

No one will call themselves Ronaldo again.

A DIATRIBE AGAINST
CRISTIANO RONALDO

IN THIS AGE of neurosis and suspicion, the diatribe has come to be thought of as merely a more artful sort of rant. Originally the genre was one of moral instruction and wasn't at all aggressive—at least not in the hands of Epictetus, Cicero, and Seneca. When they condemned someone in public, slander never entered into it.

Cristiano Ronaldo. Thousands of people shout insults at the Real Madrid player, in every stadium he plays in. What, then, can a diatribe of the philosophical kind possibly do to injure him? Criticizing someone who's won the Ballon d'Or with not one, but two different teams is a fascinatingly wrongheaded exercise. His looks and his personality, combined with the astronomical amount of money he earns, can be something of an obstruction to clear thinking. Gracefulness and good looks are designed to provoke envy, as both he and his Russian girlfriend have committed their lives to reminding us.

What we have here is a highly productive case of narcissism. When Cristiano prepares for a free kick, he readies himself by taking those few theatrical paces back—signaling to all that something special is about to happen—and then he stands, legs astride, resembling a statue of himself. It's a pose Apollo might have pulled off, had he simply practiced more. But does it actually make for a better free kick? Of course it does; drawing attention to himself is Narcissus's way of concentrating.

CR7, Cristiano's self-appointed nickname, suggests someone not subject to the normal laws of human nature, a cyborg or an archangel, a creature who waxes his hairlines *differently*.

Sometimes his mannerisms are shocking, but what of it? In mass culture, vanity is what works. Had Mick Jagger been a humble man, the Stones would have ended up playing in a garage somewhere.

People who have gotten close to Cristiano suggest a caring, somewhat naive individual, with a one-track mind; the game is the single thing he cares about. It hardly matters, in the end, that he worships his likeness in the mirror or that he spends his free time stroking puppies. It's the on-the-field exploits we judge a character by.

No player in modern football can match Cristiano for sheer athleticism. He goes forward in sustained bursts, putting into practice and even refining the advice Usain Bolt gave him when the pair had that little tête-à-tête in England. He's just as comfortable scoring with the boot as from a header, calling to mind a Gabriel Batistuta or an Oliver Bierhoff. He's also a dribbler *par excellence* and will suddenly halt mid-run, a lesson for the opposition player: you pay for his feints and jinks with time on the orthopedic bench.

All of these traits combine to form what the Germans, with all the exactitude of their language, would call a *Kraftpaket*: a powerhouse. If he were in the Olympics, he'd be at the top of the podium every time. But football is more than just a sport. Cristiano's greatness lies in far more than his physical condition; cunning and guile can't be acquired in any gym.

The masterpieces of this art have been wrought by the crippled legs of Garrincha; by tiny Lionel Messi; by the other Ronaldo, the overweight one; by Tostão, who could see only a few feet in front of him; and by Dino Zoff, the all-but-immobile Italian goalkeeper. Greatness, in this ambit, defies any of the normal means for assessing greatness. How to measure a feint, how to weigh up intuition? Or a pass into space, or a cool head, or a player's superior positional sense, or knowing exactly what your opponent is about to do?

In Cristiano's view, football is a high-performance sport, one in which personal bests come above the ability to enchant. Incapable of identifying with other players, he finds his only reflection in the object of desire: the ball. Cruyff's legacy was his introduction of the passing game, showing us that the ball ought to be the thing in motion, doing the work. CR7 seeks to reverse this certainty, supplanting the ball as the most looked-at, and most coveted, thing on the pitch.

He forgets he's taking part in one of the strangest of all permutations of public life. In a world where families are dysfunctional and residents' associations reveal to us the true strangeness of our fellow human beings, football proposes something quite unusual: human beings—eleven players—actually getting along.

Cristiano's participation is like that of a distinguished stepchild, standing out from the rest of the family. He's famous for not celebrating goals he hasn't had a hand in; his individual achievements always come above those of the group. No wonder his teammates have nicknamed him "Ansias"—anxious for it, wanting, eager beaver. His thirst for success begins and ends with him.

In the 2011–12 season, Cristiano was nominated for the Ballon d'Or. Florentino Pérez, the Real Madrid president, didn't go to the award ceremony in Monte Carlo, but his opposite number, Sandro Rosell of FC Barcelona, did. Messi won that year, and Cristiano felt he'd been scorned. In the following game, against Granada, he scored two goals but didn't celebrate. When he was asked about this show of apathy, he said he was sad "for professional reasons."

A top football player earns millions. Some of this fortune is given over to guaranteeing his public happiness; he's under contract to transmit contentment. So scoring and then making a show as if to say it's all a fraud is like flipping the bird when the crowd cheers for you. Everyone's allowed to feel depressed sometimes, but Cristiano's depression took the form of a professional "fuck you." It didn't bother him if his team lost, but if UEFA and its president didn't value him as highly as he valued himself, heaven help them.

When Cristiano arrived at Real Madrid, José Mourinho, the most sibylline manager of all time, began picking teams with a marked preference for players represented by his agent, Jorge Mendes. Never has a promoter had so much sway within a sporting entity. In order to fine-tune the tension in the squad and reinforce his fear-based authority, Mou the Terrible would sometimes criticize his favorites in public or leave them out of the starting lineup. When Cristiano's turn came, he reacted by kicking the dressing-room furniture around. Sergio Ramos and Iker Casillas made a show of support—the team captains making a brave stand against the tyrant. And what did the Apollo of Bernebéu have to say about this? He called up his agent and asked him to talk to Mourinho on his behalf. Mendes bargained with the manager, winning protection for Cristiano—problem solved (for Cristiano, that is; the rest of the group continued to have a torrid time under Mourinho).

When Marcelo refused to join the Mendes stable, arguing that the agent was like family, Cristiano stopped being friends with Marcelo and went out and praised Fabio Coentrão in the press, a recent, costly addition to the club, the most flawed player of Mourinho's tenure, and someone who happened to play in Marcelo's position.

CR7's motivations are rarely what can be called companionable. Depending on the manager, this becomes more or less marked. Anyone wishing to find out more about the Whites' dark days under Mourinho need look no further than Diego Torres's insider account, *Prepárense para perder*.[*]

---

[*] "Prepare to Lose," Ediciones B, 2013.

Ansias, prodigiously independent, prefers tactics that don't depend on the team functioning as a unit. The threat he generates in making solo runs, or from dead-ball situations, mean it's less important to keep possession of the ball; like a superhero, he'll win the war on his own.

In 2014, on receiving his second Ballon d'Or, he surprised the world with tears of gratitude. The gesture did show a human side, but the fact is it was a personal achievement that had moved him.

When Eric Cantona was asked to pick the best thing he'd ever done on a football pitch, he chose an assist he once made, thereby underlining every player's interconnection with his teammates. Even the most capricious prodigy needs the rest of the team. When Maradona went on his famous run in the 1986 World Cup in Mexico, slaloming subjects of the English crown as though they weren't there, the whole thing was made possible because Jorge Valdano was ghosting along on a parallel run, drawing numerous defenders out of Maradona's path.

Criticizing Cristiano's looks, his personality, his team, or even the money he earns—all of this is the diatribe at its most vulgar. This formidable Portuguese athlete challenges us to come up with a more complex form of condemnation. So here's the crux: no teammate of Cristiano's has ever improved by playing alongside him. A consummate egoist, the notion of the duo doesn't enter his thoughts. Careca surpassed himself playing alongside Maradona; the same with Rivellino alongside Pelé. The Brazilian poet Vinícius de Moraes had a line about the nonsense word "Clodoaldo" "rhyming with"—that is, improving in the presence of—the finer-sounding "Everaldo"; the importance of collaboration in the game cannot be overstated.

Paradoxically, the footballer who has benefited most from Cristiano is his archrival Lionel Messi. The bitter competitiveness of a single player, the vying for individual records of every kind, has spurred the Argentine to greater heights.

Cristiano's physical perfection is a mirror for his solitude on the pitch. The greatest of sorcerers have accomplices, even making use of their defects.

On a bronze plaque mounted inside the pedestal of the Statue of Liberty, the poem by Emma Lazarus welcomes those who have no capital city but their hopes:

> *Give me your tired, your poor,*
> *Your huddled masses yearning to breathe free,*
> *The wretched refuse of your teeming shore.*
> *Send these, the homeless, tempest-tost to me,*
> *I lift my lamp beside the golden door...*

Those miners who, leaving the pit, kick a ball between them, are not so different. Consummately democratic, football was dreamed up as a way of overcoming the tyranny of great athletes and giving the barefoot players a chance; with a little guile, they might overcome the limitations life has placed on them.

The pariahs that have made this terrain their own have had names such as Maradona, Di Stéfano, Puskás, Cruyff and Pelé... None of these outlandish characters relied on sheer power or pace alone, and each of them made their friends better players.

In this game, which allows for so much magic and wonder, Cristiano Ronaldo merely plays a sport.

LIONEL MESSI:
CHILDHOOD PREFIGURATIONS

NOT LONG BEFORE taking part in his first final in youth competitions, Lionel Messi got locked in a bathroom. The child whom no defender was able to stop found himself up against a broken lock. The match was about to get underway and Leo banged and banged on the door, but no one heard him. The trophy for winning this particular championship was the greatest imaginable: a bicycle.

Some would have given in to tears and resignation, and others would have been pleased to get out of the match. Leo smashed the window and jumped out. When he went out onto the pitch it was with the feeling that no one could stop him. He scored a hat trick in that final. The genius had his bicycle.

Messi's destiny has happened at least twice. He was born to Celia and Jorge in Rosario, in the Argentine province of Santa Fe, on St. John's Day in 1987, but his coming was foreshadowed at the discussions around the "good man's table" at the El Cairo café, presided over by the great cartoonist and writer Roberto Fontanarrosa. Argentina is a veritable factory of talented players, each of them already dreamed up by the most talkative storytelling fans on the planet.

After reading Macedonio Fernández's assertion that to live is a matter of distracting oneself from dying, Fontanarrosa wrote the short story "An Argentine's Heaven," in which a few friends have a barbecue and talk about football. Then they suddenly notice that they're dead. And this makes them all very happy; if they've died and they're there eating barbecued meat and discussing the match, that means they must be in heaven.

Rosario is the city of César Luis Menotti and Marcelo Bielsa, two of the great pitchside rhetoricians. Nowhere else in the world are there two sets of fans with such unswerving bitterness. Not for nothing do they accept their own disparaging nicknames: Rosario Central is known as the *Canallas*, or "Scum," and Newell's Old Boys are the *Leprosos*—"Lepers." I once mentioned to a taxi driver in Buenos Aires that I'd been to a match between Boca Juniors and River Plate. "That's nothing," he said. "We *really* hate each other." Clearly he was from Rosario.

If the spirit of Pamplona is expressed in the San Fermín running of the bulls and that of Rio de Janeiro in Carnival, in Rosario it's the unique ritual of Poy's Dive. On December 19, 1971, the Rosario Central striker Aldo Pedro Poy leaped into the air to head the ball past the Newell's keeper. They repeat that glorious moment every December 19. "I don't have any problem 'doing the deed,'" said Poy in his retirement. "The thing now is getting it up to begin with."

In the city of Che Guevara, Fito Páez, and other nonconformists, Lionel Messi was only five when he began to dazzle with a ball at his feet. He had a unique ability, but one that was also the fulfillment of a collective dream.

Leo first turned out for Grandoli, the team of his local barrio. The first man to train him was Salvador Aparicio. At sixty years of age, any number of colts had passed through Aparicio's paddock. The tiny child didn't look much, but when Aparicio saw him on the ball, his only technical advice to the others was "Kick him!" Messi could run the length of the pitch without the ball leaving his feet.

The Flea wasn't so much a little goal machine as a "hook," which is to say a gale that blew through the pitch, clearing adversaries out of the way so that one of his teammates could get on with the task—historically considered vulgar in Argentina—of putting the ball in the back of the net.

Videos from the time show a bonsai version of the current-day Messi: the same brilliance at making surging runs, the same sudden change of pace, and the same unbridled joy when he scored. As the Mexican psychoanalyst Santiago Ramírez put it: "One's fate is contained in childhood."

When he was eight his classmates lined him up in the middle in the school photo. His charisma was based on his feats with the ball, but also on that mischievous glint in his eye. A shy boy, he wasn't in fact that much of a prankster, but he had the waggish manner of someone who is always *thinking up* pranks.

His mother says he was spoiled, and there's nothing to suggest he hasn't always had people's affection. But that didn't mean destiny wouldn't have a few tests in store for him.

Messi's whole life has been a question of scale. He was eight when his parents began worrying about his size. Tests revealed that he lacked a certain growth hormone. There was a treatment, but it cost an utterly unaffordable fifteen hundred dollars a month. Two companies in Rosario lent their support, and Leo began having to inject himself once a day, showing a presence of mind you don't usually associate with children under the age of ten. From then on, the only thing that has outweighed his skill has been his determination.

After two years the money for the injections dried up. Newell's Old Boys refused to shoulder the cost, and the Messi family traveled to Buenos Aires to see if River Plate would take him on. He was the smallest amongst the children trying out and the last to be introduced into the match; there were only two minutes to go, but Leo still managed to make his mark. "Who's the father?" asked the youth coach in charge that day. Jorge Messi stepped forward. "He stays," said the coach.

But he never won a contract. The club with the red stripes didn't want to enter into negotiations over the transfer with Newell's, or take on the medical costs, for a player of indisputable talent but no guarantees as to what he might become.

Rosario is where Messi would have liked to stay, there where the slow ships advance up the River Paraná, and it was where his friends were, where they would all celebrate "Leper Day" together. Sentimental bonds are good for a football player.

There's nobody more motivated—or anything more scarce—than a player who is also a fan of the team he plays for.

Juan Román Riquelme was one of the game's great stay-homers; he felt at home in Boca's pulsating stadium, and when he put on another team's colors all his powers deserted him. Messi wanted to stay on, too, but his fate was to become a nomad in extremis, at the opposite end of the spectrum from Riquelme.

He crossed the seas in 2000 to try out with Barcelona. The blaugrana are "more than a club." Did that mean they would adopt this curious Rosario great, this boy?

On arrival in Catalonia, there were complications. The coach, Carles Rexach, was away in Sydney. Leo and his father sat tight for a fortnight in a hotel overlooking the Plaza de España. They got to know the local area better than they would have liked, and began casting envious glances at the blue airport shuttle bus. They didn't want to stay on and were on the verge of heading home when they got the message: Rexach would be back the following day.

They say that when Rexach was coaching teams in Japan, he was so laid-back he was never sure which of the two sides playing was his. On the day of the appointment with the Messis, he arrived late and with his usual distracted air. He easily spotted the miniature Argentine out on the pitch. "Sign him up," he said, without a moment's hesitation. And he wasn't a man to doubt. "He spent fifteen days in Barcelona," said Rexach, "and one would have been enough!"

To put the family's mind at ease, the coach signed the thinnest "contract" in football. On December 14, 2000 he took a napkin from the bar and wrote a promise to watch over the boy. As a document it had as much legal force as the multitudinous prayers uttered at Montserrat, Catalonia's sacred mountain, and is today housed in the office of Josep Maria Minguella, the recruitment manager, on display as an extremely valuable piece of popular art.

On March 1, 2001 a proper contract was signed, and the Messi family moved to Barcelona to support the Flea.

One of the greatest challenges in the life of a professional footballer is dealing with so much solitude; an eternity of tedium in hotel rooms needs dispatching. The situation is exacerbated when the player in question is very young and far from home. Deprived of his usual pastimes and his mother's cooking, Leo discovered Barcelona to be a place as boring as sucking nails.

His siblings also began to feel depressed, and the mother decided to take them back to Argentina. Leo stayed there with his father, in a city where at the time another foreigner was growing older: the albino gorilla Snowflake.

THE IMPORTANCE OF STAYING ON

Messi was a supreme natural talent, but the history of the game is littered with talented players who never made it. Was it worth staying on in Barcelona, far from family, with no guarantees about how things would pan out? Sometimes Leo shut himself in the bathroom so he could cry without his father seeing him.

One evening Jorge Messi decided he'd had enough, and suggested they head home. Another door appeared to be shutting on the player's career. But at the age of thirteen Leo was already a specialist in adversity. The boy who escaped through a window to win his first title said he wanted to stay on; everyone they knew was in Rosario, but Barcelona had La Masia, the football academy that had produced Xavi, Iniesta, and Guardiola.

Incapable of socializing, Leo was always the last to arrive in the cafeteria and would sit over to one side where he didn't have to talk to anyone. He tried to avoid the fish and salad they served and took all the time in the world over the things he liked (the meat, the chips, any kind of pasta). Leonardo Faccio, who managed to write a very interesting book about this near-unexplorable character, said this: "Without the ball at his feet, Leo Messi resembles a clone of the electrifying player we all know and love—with the batteries taken out. A poor representative of who he really is." And this was true from his very first day at La Masia, where he would light up the pitch and then, away from it, show signs of distraction and boredom.

Rexach was generous enough to sign a player who would never play for him. He didn't stay on long enough to see Messi's debut from the Barca dugout.

That honor would go to Frank Rijkaard, who had brought Messi through at a measured pace and put an arm around his shoulder after his first serious injury. After Rijkaard Messi played for Guardiola, who interpreted the value of youth in football better than any other coach; he had a profound personal knowledge of the Masia experience, of the solitary tribulations compensated for by sleeping with a view of Camp Nou from your window.

Guardiola's first-ever job at the stadium was as a ball boy, and he worked his way up from there to become the club's manager. At the start of the 2009–10 season, seeing limitations in his squad, he said, "We'll use the kids," in reference to Sergio Busquets and Pedro. With Guardiola in the dugout, Messi was sure of a place.

Twenty-six years of age at the time of writing, he has become the most admired player on the planet. Game in, game out, he demonstrates how resistant to logic this game is, how the physical is anything but the defining factor: being five foot six did nothing to stop him from scoring a winning header—beating the giant Man Utd keeper Edwin van der Sar—in the Champions League final.

His hallmark is receiving the ball outside the area, stopping dead, starting off on a lateral scamper, leaving a couple of defenders in his wake, and having a shot. Though he also comes up with goals that have gone down as emblems of footballing craft: sealing Barca's sixth consecutive title with a chested effort and scoring against Arsenal by flipping the ball up to himself—not once but twice—in the area, before beating the bamboozled keeper.

Hernán Casciari came up with a memorable comparison: Messi is like a dog that won't let go of the sponge. Ever. Though he is a dog also happy to be involved in the continuous struggle for the ball. Messi pursues the ball as though there were no other thing in life, ignoring the kicks and fouls, carrying on in the direction of his only goal. Like the puppy that is happy just to be expending energy, Barca's number 10 is a complete stranger to taking a break, let alone giving in.

Sometimes referees are too mesmerized by his skill to award the fouls that come raining in, and because they believe that even if he falls, he's still able to finish off the move.

There's a documentary with Picasso painting a bull for the camera. The lines advance with unsettling virtuosity, until the work is perfect. But since the camera keeps on rolling, the artist doesn't stop there and starts adding in unnecessary details. He becomes excessive, and the director doesn't dare stop him. Who's going to interrupt a genius in a state of grace? So it is with Messi. Blowing up for a foul seems like an attack, equivalent to throwing something onstage during a concert. The opposition may be placing illegal objects in Leo's path, but the ref has been taken out altogether.

Leo Messi has taken football to belief-defying heights. Rapt, the ref becomes like us, the spectators: a mute witness to a passing sort of glory.

IS THERE ANYONE THERE?

Messi's well-known strong points contrast with the life he leads in private. This most brilliant of players seems oblivious to the thrills and spills of an imaginative inner life. He comes from a country that does melodrama better than anyone, with its tango and its high concentration of psychoanalysts, a nation where having neuroses is a way of demonstrating your eloquence and where an Under-17 player is quite capable of using terms like "trauma" and "taboo," and knowing what they're talking about. Yet Messi seems resistant to the mysteries of the unconscious. Someone making a TV ad tried to get inside his intimate inner world, asking what he did in the changing room before an important match. "I chew gum," came his devastating response.

And it isn't just that he's reserved, it's that he appears at peace with being silent. When he isn't on the pitch or with his girlfriend, he applies himself to a certain pastime with a monk-like dedication: the siesta. He can do a two- or three-hour stretch after lunch, and it doesn't stop him getting ten hours in at night.

Everything he does away from the pitch, he does slowly. Leonardo Faccio tells an anecdote about a party during Messi's time at primary school: one of his teachers gave him a snail costume.

A genius who celebrates his life by sleeping. This might seem strange on this exhibitionist planet of ours, where celebrities applaud their own success in the company of Slovenian models, spending time aboard yachts of tremendous length, or getting their premolars encrusted with diamonds.

The material and spiritual ambitions of Lionel Messi stretch no further than a ball at his feet, a family around him, a woman by his side, and a nice blanket to lie down under. Isn't it too, well, simple? Especially seeing as we've all bought into the dramatic pedagogical idea that talent always has its roots in some kind of pain?

The 2011 Oscars honored two films that centered on sensitive, impaired souls: *The King's Speech* with its stuttering King of England, and *Black Swan*, with its schizophrenic ballerina. We have an easier time accepting excellence if we know it originates in some kind of suffering that had to be overcome: the skater gliding along with supreme grace, though she is blind.

Some sort of torment, the wound necessary for talent to emerge, mitigates the excessive brilliance of a genius. We delight in the results and at the same time feel thankful that we didn't have to go through all the pain necessary to achieve them.

Messi, with the growth-hormone injections and the initial solitude of his arrival in Barcelona, has hardly been exempt from misery. But it still feels almost scandalous for him to be so boring before and after the whistle blows. "He can't be that *normal!*" complain the journalists, anxious to uncover the anomaly, the strange proclivity, the whitefly, as the saying goes, nestled in the brain of the champion.

Emotional autism is one of the least serious of the charges leveled by these inquisitors. Like Forrest Gump, the Argentine 10 is seen as a record-smashing simpleton who only needs a nod from the manager to do astonishing things on the pitch. "Run Forrest, run."

Messi goes to sleep with a book, and has no desire to see the Taj Mahal. When he had to choose a tattoo, it wasn't a Che face he went for, like Maradona, but an image of his mother. Each time he scores a goal, he points to the sky in memory of his grandmother. The horizon of his myths is formed by his family; this is what makes him normal. Is there some defect that sets him apart? Celebrities tend to dedicate themselves to consumerism—a vice we can forgive. For someone at the top of all the stats tables, what could be more normal than excess. So extreme acquisitiveness "humanizes" the famous person: he amasses an increasing number of works of art, more children, more stunning models, more classic cars and pointless hats— more of everything than his fellow beings who have a mortgage to pay.

To be normal in the recently fashionable way, Leo could employ a PR expert to buy extravagant things in his name. If only he owned sixteen life-size ceramic giraffes, all questions about his "simplicity" would cease.

Like all stars who dedicate a large part of their time to making commercials, he has a double who gets caught in the rain on camera so he can be saved from a cold. Faccio says that Leo became concerned that this alter ego, the one signing autographs and going to clubs, might be moving to center stage; he's so shy that his double has to be as well.

Save vague suggestions about the occasional orgy in his Puerto Madero apartment—something not all that strange in the primitive world of football—he's also not well known for his blowouts.

Human beings like asking themselves improbable questions that don't always have that much of a bearing on their lives: "Is there life on Mars?" "Is there a God?" "Does Messi have an unconscious?"

He's gotten up after so many rough tackles without complaint that it makes him seem immune to inner turbulence. But then in the summer of 2011 we began to see some unusually visceral reactions. The young lion does know how to roar.

THE MYSTERY OF THE TEASPOON

After losing 5–0 in the "first leg" of the 2010–11 Real Madrid-Barca clásico, Jose Mourinho rang the tactical changes for the "return." In the run-up to this devastating loss, he'd created a wrecking ball of a team, bashing aside opponents far more quickly than the Catalan side (who always prefer delivering death by a thousand cuts).

The Portuguese is not a defensive coach. He brings out the best in every squad he manages and only parks the bus when he determines it to be the only route to victory—when he judges the opposition superior. This was what he did as manager of Inter in the 2010 Champions League semifinal they played against Barcelona.

Spain's La Liga has become a metaphor for a country in crisis; only two or three ever stand a realistic chance of coming out on top, and there are always eight or nine struggling to avoid relegation. The most intense—and democratic—passion awoken isn't about success but about saving yourself from utter disaster.

The "Merengue" hurricane was tearing through teams in 2010, but no one knew if they could do the same to Barca. Partly it was a question of tactics; the *azulgrana*'s game was based on possession of the ball, whereas this Madrid side only needed the ball for a matter of seconds to create danger. Two opposing languages faced off in the November chill. And we know what happened next: Real went out onto the pitch not only the color of ghosts, but with a similarly flimsy attitude.

Barca doled out a lesson. A rumor went around that Wayne Rooney's wife, watching the match at their home in Manchester, surprised the Man Utd player by standing and applauding the performance. "I've made peace with my profession," said the English striker, enthused by the Catalan concerto.

For the "return leg," Mourinho needed to come up with a strategy that Rooney would not celebrate. He didn't care in the slightest about the quality of the spectacle. The Portuguese's competitive streak brooks no style arguments.

A destructive game plan needs an accomplice: the ref. Many are the difficult decisions that have to be made by this troubled, sweating man. Clear leg breakers are not difficult to decide about, but other fouls, less crass, not so obviously violent, are less easy. A little tug on a shirt, a nudge to knock someone off balance, dives—none of these are direct attempts on the opposition, though they do affect them. Messi was subjected to more than ten such aggressions in each of the two matches.

César Luis Menotti has pointed out, rightly, that the principal thing that holds a game up is repeat fouls. You shouldn't have to mutilate a player to be shown a card.

The return was at the Bernebéu, and Mourinho put a defender in midfield; Pepe was charged with man-marking Messi. It was a match played in front of a safety-deposit box: not only must the Camp Nou thrashing be avoided, but football as well. In the midst of what became a foul festival, something happened that had never happened before: Leo became exasperated. Like a caged animal, he kicked a publicity hoarding. Pepe went over and, tapping his shaved head provocatively, said "Lost your mind?" The pursuer diagnosing paranoia.

But in fact Messi was very much using his head. He used it to get fed up. Whoever says he doesn't get affected by things ought to remember that moment, a moment when he was made to feel powerless.

He kicked a hoarding on another occasion, at Wembley, in his second Champions League final—though this time it was an expression of euphoria.

On May 28, 2011 he looked possessed when he wheeled away after scoring; he was impelled by an enraged, exasperated joy. He left the print of his orange boot on some commercial product or other. The treatment of Pepe the Destroyer and the nobility of Manchester United at Wembley brought him to boiling point. His emotions aren't a *terra incognita* awaiting cartographers; he simply doesn't express them very often.

How to tell if someone who's usually very quiet is saying nothing because they're annoyed? Messi's interests may be limited, but he gets annoyed should any of them be obstructed. The worse thing, in his eyes, is not starting a match when he's fit. The idea that he's being "kept back" for another game makes him feel like a grandmother's dress—like he's being mothballed.

According to the *El País* writer Ramon Besa, when Guardiola put Messi on the bench in a match against Sevilla (the previous time they played, Barca had won 4–0), the Flea didn't show up at the following training session. Messi's teammate, Besa, says:

"Thought he must have had a cold, or that something unforeseen had come up. As it turned out, Messi was angry at not having been picked, and it wasn't until the following morning that the feeling passed—in the same way as it had arrived, without Messi knowing exactly why."

On another occasion, he took part in a training session with a plastic spoon in his mouth. He hadn't just left the object at the coffee bar. A strange sign. The rest of the team felt obliged to examine their consciences: Who had failed to pass him the ball? Who had accidentally injured him? Who had not won the ball back when he needed it?

When the best player on Earth trains with a small spoon between his lips, alarm bells ring in the same way as when a tenor goes out to sing with a thermometer in his mouth.

After a few minutes the genius spat out the piece of cutlery. Crisis over.

The person who has best studied Lionel Messi's reactions is Pep Guardiola. I had lunch with him in December 2012, along with his great friend David Trueba and a couple of journalist friends.

Guardiola is a fan of forays out into the strange world of not-training sessions and not-press conferences—where there isn't a single objective like the match on the weekend. Though not quite as bookish as the likes of Pardeza or Valdano, he likes to know what's going on in the world and reads a fair amount. Curiously, once away from the tensions of his usual environment and in the company of friends from other professions, he returns to his perpetual theme with renewed vigor. "I was never completely happy as a footballer," he said at lunch—with everyone else in the restaurant straining to catch his words. "I worried too much, I'd vomit before matches, the whole experience was agonizing." Ever since then he's had the temperament more of a strategist than of the player making things happen on the pitch. In the days when he was still wearing number 4 on his back, Valdano characterized him as a "coach with a ball at his feet."

"You have no idea how envious I am of my players. I was never able to enjoy it like they do. They're so happy out there, I want to kill them!" Some of his players are like him in their vocation as coaches: Xavi and Busquets are both such talented tacticians they won't be out of place among the dugout thinkers, whereas Messi is impossible to imagine out of the team strip. He is psychologically a creature of the present, of the goals he scores after siesta. He lacks the capacities for evocation that a commentator needs, and he isn't a forward planner, as coaches need to be. What's he going to do when he hangs up his boots? Eat steak in a mansion where the most expensive piece of furniture is the sofa?

"I'll still be in the dugout when I'm sixty," says Guardiola, happy to be involved in the part of football where he feels more at ease and that doesn't last as long. That's where he watches Messi—more closely than anyone ever has. Barca's style of play is, among other things, a mechanism to free the number 10: Samuel Eto'o and Zlatan Ibrahimović alike had to stand aside so as not to obstruct Messi's route to goal.

No one gets to be the world's best in a team sport without the complicity of teammates. Guardiola worked tirelessly to create the moves in which Messi works both as midfield axis and center forward: a number 10 mutating into a number 9.

Your average poachers have the most abrupt job in the world: they only come into play for a few seconds a game. Messi offers up a slow-burn recital on the wings, but also pops up as a feinting striker to put away a pass he even laid on for himself.

Eto'o was your classic fox in the box, an overly fixed role for Barca's *total* style. And Ibrahimović, for his part, was a giant used to ruling alone. In Serie A they'd each become used to providing the point of the attack, to resolving matters solo. Neither was able to adjust properly to Barca's gregarious schematic.

In the 2010–11 season, Guardiola brought in David Villa, with his Pedro-like ability to stretch a game. The center-forward area was freed up, and in Xavi and Iniesta they had two of the greatest providers ever to grace the game.

With these changes made, Messi, already the best in the game, began outdoing himself to an even greater degree. Guardiola knew how to break down the distinct phases of the Barcelona engine.

The azulgrana tactics, then, were arranged to suit Messi's strong points, something that has never happened when he's been on national duty. And yet the albiceleste have always been a strong priority for him. Leonardo Faccio reconstructs a little-known episode: the Flea lit up pitches in Spain from the moment he became the youngest player to score in La Liga (at the age of sixteen, against Albacete), but the shock waves of his talent took a long time to register for Argentina.

He was invited to play for the Spanish youth team at sixteen. According to FIFA rules, this would have barred him from ever playing for Argentina, so Messi declined. But then Argentina dragged their feet in calling him up. "It was five months between the call-up from Spain and the Argentine Federation getting in touch," says Faccio.

The story ought to ring alarm bells for anyone who criticizes Messi for a lack of identity. He hasn't lost his accent, or his Rosario ways, and plans on retiring back to that city—one he only ever left because he couldn't get medical treatment there.

But the schism between him and Argentine fans will always be there until he wins something with the national side. He's never played for a club in his home country, and his debt to the albiceleste feels pending. Another anecdote, this time from Johan Cruyff, is illuminating on the matter: in his Ajax days, when he went out, he'd be congratulated on the streets of Holland, whereas when he moved to Barcelona, the people would *thank* him. His achievements were seen by his compatriots as strictly professional, whereas Barcelonans felt like he'd become one of them. Lionel Messi's Argentine drama consists in the fact his countrymen don't yet feel able to thank him.

THE VIEW FROM THE TOP

The worst thing about success is the way it cancels out the pleasures contained in hoping and dreaming you will one day be successful. For a team whose cabinet is glutted with trophies, the hardest thing is retaining the desire. What's the point in striving for an objective you've already achieved?

When, at the beginning of the 2010–11 season, Barca lost to minnows Hércules CF, Guardiola had to issue a wake-up call for them to continue dreaming.

"Leo needs no special motivation," he told me at the lunch. "He competes with himself; there are always new challenges." He gave a simple but very revealing example: in one training session, Busquets went in for the ball recklessly, taking Messi out and leaving him with a gashed leg. The session went on without any further incidents. In the changing room afterward, Busquets went over to apologize, and Messi, his voice calm, pointed at the cut and gave the enigmatic answer: "This says 'Sergio Busquets.' " What did he mean? His best friends on the team, fellow Argentines Gabi Milito and Javier Mascherano, understood before the others. The Flea never forgets; there was a debt now, one he would leap across. A few days later, when everyone seemed to have forgotten the affair, Messi took Busquets out, trotting away with a mischievous smile. 1–1.

A measure of his tenacity is the targets he sets himself. When Mauricio Pochettino, in his days as manager of Espanyol, said something offhand about Messi, it just so happened that Barcelona's other team came out on the wrong end of a 5–1 drubbing in the following match. Messi celebrated a job well done by drifting over to the wing closest to the opposition dugout for the last few minutes of the game—to plant himself in Pochettino's mind for good.

And if he did need incentivizing, in the summer of 2010 along came Jose Mourinho to take the helm at Real Madrid. The effect was twofold: he motivated the Merengues with his intricate conspiracy theories but also spurred on their archrivals with his constant affronts.

It was clear from the off that Mourinho hadn't come to Spain for a popularity contest. In an early press conference, he suggested that if journalists wanted to speak to a *nice* coach, Pep Guardiola was their man, leaving his opposite number in charge of keeping La Liga civil.

The Portuguese followed through on his promise to be thoroughly unpleasant, to such a degree that the most unfathomable thing about him is his second surname: Dos Santos—or Two Saints—though perhaps heavenly algebra is such that in fact "duplicate" saints add up to Lucifer, the fallen angel...

And Mou turned out to be just the Gatorade that Messi needed. He'd have played astonishingly well if he hadn't turned up, but the Portuguese helped him rehydrate.

The team's increasing reliance on him led to an interesting paradox. In the spring of 2011 he was in competition with Cristiano Ronaldo to be top scorer in La Liga, and there was the chance he might have fallen for the temptation of seeing goals as solo victories; Mourinho's dogged twisting of Barca's strong points *helped* Messi become a more mature player. His individualism remained firmly in the locker room.

Menotti has a good line on this, the collectivization of Messi's own game:

> Messi learned. What soloists need to do is control the rhythm because, if not, they only disrupt the orchestra. And that's what he did: he'd pick up the ball and,

every time, pluck his violin three or four times, but on occasion you'd think, "*What would have happened if he'd stepped aside just then?*" And that began to become part of his thinking. He began setting other players up. There's more to him now, he takes up better positions, he'll return a pass as if to say, "*You go for it, there was nothing on for me then.*" Before he was always looking to go and win the match on his own, but not anymore. He evolved. And that's where you get a sense of the impact of the maestro: What would have happened with these players if not for Pep?

Messi's competitiveness is borne out by one strange statistic: he commits more fouls than other technical players. In four neurotic games between Barca and Madrid, he was responsible for fourteen of his team's sixty-eight infractions, an unheard-of quota for a player of such finesse in his position.

In short, this boy-faced genius doesn't lack substance. Though it takes a little patience if you want to see them, he does have his outbursts. He might not be one to air them on crappy daytime TV, and you're not going to catch him throwing his phone out the window, but the things that annoy him and the things he takes satisfaction in do affect his mood. What Guardiola would look out for in him, in terms of emotions, was that glint in his eye, that spark of malice; if that was there, all was well.

In South Africa 2010 he had an altogether different coach. Maradona's way in the dugout was to try and transmit his charisma: training sessions with him involved more kisses and hugs than argumentation. Intelligently enough, Maradona made Messi's roommate Verón, a veteran whose experiences might conceivably rub off. But Messi isn't out there looking to run the show. His imagination makes him a central player, but it isn't his natural setting to come up with what other players ought to do, or to make their decisions. Maradona giving him the captain's armband wasn't a favor by any means—rather, it was akin to a father taking his son to a brothel to instantly make a man of him. But the extra pressure weighed on Messi, a player who still had something childlike in his game, who appeals for support with his tattoos of mother and grandmother. Maradona offered him the historical opportunity to become his successor, but that's not Messi. He was comfortable in the Guardiola cocoon, but he withered at Maradona's shove.

The next date with destiny was Brazil 2014. Triumph there, and the facts would justify everything that had happened to date; we'd all say that Messi needed to go to the home of Argentina's greatest enemy in order to win his greatest trophy.

Leo was older now, and a more complete player. He was eighteen when, in 2005, he was named best player at the U-20 World Cup, and when he scored his first goal for Barcelona. On March 10, 2007, in the Bernebéu, he confirmed his place at the pinnacle, with his hat trick in the clásico.

The numbers worn by Messi attest to his path to becoming an idol. He made his debut for Barcelona with 30 on his back, became 19 as he moved up from the youth ranks, before the definitive upgrade, the number 10 made sacred by Maradona and Pelé, and that he had worn as a boy playing in the red and black of Newell's.

In 2007, against Getafe, he came up with his double of Maradona's 1986 goal against England. That feat confirmed his talent; all he had to do then was repeat it. The deluge of goals and the six titles he won with Barca in the 2008–09 season brought him the Ballon d'Or, and when he went up to collect the trophy he smiled like a child in an ice-cream shop. But he wasn't content to stop there, and in 2009–10 equaled Ronaldo's emphatic forty-seven goals.

Other difficult-to-believe records were still to come. He became a headache for the team of the aspirin makers, Bayer Leverkusen, with his five goals against them in 2012—a Champions League high. And in the same year he broke a record that had stood for forty years: Gerd Muller's eighty-five goals in a calendar year. Messi visited "Der Bomber" with a signed shirt. Prizes have become just part of the job for Messi. It seemed in many ways quite normal that he should win the Ballon d'Or four times, surpassing three-time winners Platini, Cruyff, and van Basten in doing so.

It hit Messi hard when Guardiola left Barcelona in 2012. The coach who had done everything possible to help him realize his talent, even foregoing a center forward so that Messi could be two players at once—initiating moves as a winger and finishing them off as a striker—took a sabbatical after four grueling seasons. Grueling and successful: with Messi's assistance, he'd won fourteen of the available nineteen titles during that time.

Messi didn't attend the farewell conference because he didn't want to cry in public. But his performance level didn't dip with the master's departure; in fact he only got better under Tito Vilanova, an in-house appointment of Guardiola's right-hand man, one to carry on the project.

As well as his trademark moves, he'll also go down as having invented goals of great symbolic artifice, as in 2008–09 when he sealed Barca's league victory with a chested goal.

On April 10, 2013, Messi revolutionized the game—again. He was injured and couldn't start in the match against Paris Saint Germain, but with Barca losing 1–0 he had to be thrown into the fray. He came on sixteen minutes into the second half, and it was a watershed; PSG waned and Barca had a resurgence. The emotional state of the stadium changed. Messi's impact goes beyond merely footballing: it is spiritual. Though he could hardly move, his presence changed things. He laid on an assist and Barca ended up drawing, good enough to see them through to the next round. It was the first time that Messi had played in soul rather than in body. It was a glimpse, in a way, of what his legacy will be; when he retires, the mere memory of him will help the team to win matches. As the Brazilian commentator Nelson Rodrigues put it: "Even ghosts have a duty to their club."

As long as he continues playing, there's no way of knowing where he'll get to. All we know is that just as no lock exists that will stop him, no defense does either.

When a child wants a bike, there's a lot he'll do to get it. When a man plays like a child who wants a bike, that's the best player in the world.

BLOOD ON THE TERRACES: VIOLENCE IN THE BUSINESS OF FIFA

ONE OF THE STRANGEST THINGS about Western democracies is the way they've cordoned off the primitive impulse. And the place it's been cordoned off? Professional sport. The same countries that preach about the rule of law and accountability accept the presence of institutions that are, strictly speaking, criminal enclaves. The most renowned is the one known as "FIFA."

Utterly divorced from fiscal transparency, specializing in the peddling of influence and shady dealings, a levier of kickbacks, and an ally of autocratic governments, football's chief global proponent has realized a dream of conducting itself like an irascible banana republic within the realms of the free market. With more paid-up members than the UN, this international organism is run by a group of people only interested in satisfying their own cravings and caprice.

Sport is a strange universe of political longevity—where João Havelange can spend twenty-four years at the helm in FIFA, Antonio Samaranch twenty-one years running the International Olympic Committee, and José Sulaimán more than three decades as president of the World Boxing Council.

With seventeen years as FIFA president, Sepp Blatter could be seen as something of a Johnny-come-lately in the sporting mafia, a mere apprentice in this patriarchal order. But that hasn't stopped him from bringing the game into disrepute. The fact that the coming World Cups are going to be held in Russia and Qatar—Qatar particularly—casts serious doubts on an institution that cares little about what is going on inside a country *as long as the business does alright.*

Sheltering behind the ideology of "fair play," FIFA bows down before one god and one god only: sponsorship deals. Brazil outlawed alcohol in all of its stadiums at the start of the 2000s, yet FIFA forced Budweiser to be made available there during the last World Cup. Though of dubious drinkability, this "beer" was given the go-ahead to contravene local laws, because it put money in FIFA's pockets as an official sponsor.

The body's record on jurisprudence looks like something out of a Borgia intrigue. On the eve of Italia '90, Mexico tried one of its many sporting impostures by falsifying several players' dates of birth so they could take part in a youth tournament. Though the crime was in the amateur realm, the senior team bore the consequences: their passport to the World Cup—they'd already qualified—was revoked. The lucky beneficiary of this was the team that had come behind Mexico in qualification: the US.

To what did this unexpected guest owe its invitation? This exemplary FIFA penalty was designed not only to exclude Mexico, but also to "warm up" the American environment ahead of the subsequent World Cup—USA '94. At the time football was seen, stateside, as a fake sport, a sport for girls. The Mexican Federation's reward for not kicking up a fuss comprised several cushy jobs for its staff, and some mouthwatering deals for the TV networks.

I covered Italia '90 for the newspaper *El Nacional* and was surprised to find that the second most numerous TV delegation, after the Italians, was Mexican, even though their own team wasn't there to report on. The explanation for this is that the Mexican Football Federation was for a long time run by a man named Guillermo Cañeda, who was also vice president of the TV company Televisa. In other words, the men who run our national game accepted losing out on the football in exchange for winning TV rights.

The men in charge are a paradoxical bunch, acting like gangsters but claiming their crimes are for the good of the people. For a long time, Julio Grondona and his close relations dominated Argentine football like something out of *The Sopranos*; a perpetrator of genocide in Serbia, Slobodan Milošević, employed Ultras from Red Star Belgrade in repressive military maneuvers; and in Italy Silvio Berlusconi, bathing in the reflected glory of the club he owned, AC Milan, assumed the presidency of the country whilst mouthing an Azzurri anthem: "Forza Italia."

It's a strange task that falls to the twenty-two men running around on the pitch; really they're just there to allow the high-powered executives, way up in the members' boxes, to do a little business.

THE FAN: A MARTYR TO HOPE

Footballing authorities are often above the law. This being so, how can they expect to tell fans to behave well? At what point does patience run out in the man who shows up to *support* his team? If FIFA's general practice is to avoid the law, fans might feel quite justified in taking it into their own hands.

Adolfo Bioy Casares once wrote that any supporter whose team is a perennial loser is in for a wonderful lesson in stoicism. Fans of a losing side get a repeat tutorial in the noble sense of resignation. Certain chants endorse the sense of the greatness of misfortune, like Real Betis's "*Viva el Betis, manque pierda*" ("Long live Betis, even in loss") or the "*aunque gane*" of Atlas: "[We support them] even in victory." These fans know full well that the final score isn't everything and that the trophy cabinet isn't the only place where achievements are tallied up. For them sport has more to do with a sense of belonging than with winning or losing; they aren't in hock to vulgar success.

Even Brazil went through a barren spell once, and when they appeared set to shake off their losing trance, having booked their place in the World Cup Final in 1950 on home turf, Uruguay batted them aside. The great commentator Nelson Rodrigues talked about them having a "street-dog complex"—they'd never get to sleep the triumphant siesta of the domestic dog.

After the "Maracanãzo" defeat, Brazil changed their strip from their customary white, like they were shedding their skin to shuffle off a curse. After this transfiguration, dressed in the yellow, blue, and green, they went on to win World Cup after World Cup; the point being that all their victories were fed by the desperation, patience, and pain of a fan base that had lost everything for several decades—everything except hope.

The same might be said of Barcelona's victim complex and the way it ended when Johan Cruyff took up his place in the dugout. A period of blaugrana dominance had the added value of being preceded by so many defeats.

Does football contain any specific keys for understanding violence in general? It doesn't lead to violence, it sublimates it—via an "unarmed army," as the unforgettable Spanish writer Manuel Vázquez Montalbán liked to say. So how to account for the occasional outbreak of violence in stadiums? It's a bipolar world in which the people making the rules do anything they can to dodge legalities, at the same time demanding stoical resignation from supporters. The guys at the top have the ability to put a player up for sale—utterly arbitrarily, and even if the supporters love this player—and besmirch the shirt with questionable advertising, and sign agreements so that the team has to go on an arduous preseason tour in China, and accept handsome TV deals that mean the team has to play three times a week (the perfect recipe for injuries).

The logic that reigns in the private boxes is different from the logic in the stands. Two opposed worlds exist in a tension—aggravated by social conflict and sporting disaster. As a mirror for society, football condenses and steps up the life outside of the stadium. In 1969, the war between Honduras and El Salvador coincided with a match between the nations' teams, and no one was thinking about the final score. It wasn't the destiny of the ball that was in play, but the poisoned relations between these two neighboring countries.

Which is usually the case as well when it comes to football violence. The Heysel tragedy in the 1985 European Cup Final between Liverpool and Juventus had more to do with deep dislocations in English society, which also happened to be the spawning ground for hooliganism, than anything that happened on the pitch or the penalty Platini scored for Juve.

PITCHES UNDER CLOSE SURVEILLANCE

The incidences of violence that have tarnished our stadiums point to a crisis. Moments where individuals act in concert with other individuals allow for tensions to be vented, but these tensions don't necessarily have anything to do with the acts themselves. Ortega y Gasset's view was that sport gives human beings a holiday from civilization. Small doses of the primitive can be a great valve for the pressures of modern life. The crowds that gather around a pitch for a big match bring back something of the tribal hordes from the very beginnings of our species.

There's nothing offensive about this as long as the representation of the emotions remains out there on the pitch. The fan with the face paint, chanting whatever he chants, is not a violent figure *per se*; he accepts the result, whatever it may be, and the only thing he does to affect the outcome is to shout as loudly as his voice box will allow.

The problem is that certain chants do not confine themselves to the expulsion of impassioned air from the lungs and demand actual retaliation—especially if they are xenophobic, discriminatory, nationalist, misogynistic, or homophobic. Given that there are as many different kinds of prejudice in the world as there are people, some forms of discrimination become quite highly specialized: fans of a club in a certain neighborhood find it within themselves to call a rival side, whose stadium is at the south end of the same street as theirs, "Africans."

For years, ultras within certain clubs have been not only tolerated but also supported by executives. If the people in charge of the game cannot be examples of probity, how are the fans going to be? If the people around Messi dodge taxes for the "good" of a player whose only motivation is goals, what kind of behavior can be expected of the fan on the dole?

Some maniacs can be stopped by surveillance and control measures, but the real issue is something else. Spotting someone making fascist signs behind a goal, or throwing a pig head onto the pitch, is less important than the necessary changes in a society where such behavior begins. You don't stop cancer by popping an aspirin.

Besides, being overzealous about surveillance can just end up demonizing people's passion for the game. Welcome to the world of Big Brother, where, depending on which officer's on duty, a gesture or a certain chant can be deemed "dangerous"!

In violent groups, the violence, whether it be verbal or physical, fits within certain codes, which in turn provide a sense of belonging. And these aren't people infected by any strange virus; pernicious as it may be, their behavior does obey a certain logic. There is no such thing as misbehavior without context; anyone "misbehaving" as part of a group gains the compensatory inclusion in something transcendent, something more important to them than that context. In general, getting a swastika tattoo has less to do with a rigorous observance of the tenets of national socialism than identifying with your friend who, whether because they were disturbed, ignorant, perverse, or simply naive, already got their own swastika tattoo. I'm not trying to justify irrational sloganeering, but some attempt must be made to actually understand it.

Football is the most widely dispersed identity system on Earth. Millions of human beings are *of* certain clubs or, as in Barcelona's case, an entity that even aspires to be "more than a club." This very valuable symbolic capital comes under risk when a team stops representing its people. And therein lies modern football's most serious problem: when authority acts according to its own whims, fans begin to feel authorized to seek other things to identify with, and that may include violence.

Stuffing stadiums full of cameras and police officers is the latest victory for the authoritarianism that rules the game. Only when FIFA and the politicians and companies associated with the sport submit to democratic rules, only when these vultures within the game lose their "protected species" status (to use the apt phrase of Valencian novelist Ferran Torrent), only at that point will bloodshed on the terraces cease.

CHILDHOOD FOR SALE

André Malraux used the term "the strange age of sports" to refer to an epoch that organized entertainment on the basis of large-scale competitions.

The sports industry has become so successful that it even allows for bad things to be done in the name of good. With the sanitary pretext of creating clean minds inside Apollonian bodies, it has turned itself into a very profitable arm of organized crime.

For Juan Antonio Samaranch, the perfect autocrat, the International Olympic Committee provided the perfect front, and his embezzlements only came to light once he had moved away from the Olympic rings. In the case of Sepp Blatter, he was outed time and again by the press, and yet that did nothing to reduce his desire to squeeze money out of every last blade of grass.

The former player Luis Figo decided against taking Blatter on in the FIFA presidency elections, pointing out that there was no way he could run against a Mafiosi.

FIFA describes itself as not for profit. This ludicrous self-image allows it to maintain total fiscal opacity, the kind Al Capone would have delighted in. It isn't enough just to commit crimes; you've got to dodge a few taxes too.

The need to renovate stadiums unleashes a chain of interests that can lead to insane projects like the one in Manaus. Anyone who thought the old opera erected in those far reaches of the Amazon was crazy should have a look at the World Cup stadium there—in a place where no top division team plays. It's become a coliseum for iguanas nowadays.

Such instances will only be repeated on a grander scale in Qatar, host for the 2022 World Cup. When Henry Miller wrote *The Air-Conditioned Nightmare*, little did he know he was providing a prescient description of the arrival of football into the oil-rich sands of the Middle East.

Due to the fact the Qatari league doesn't need so many stadiums, the plan is to put up edifices that can be taken apart and sold off to other countries. Can there be anything more money-spinning than organizing the pinnacle of football in arenas where the only thing growing abundantly is cash?

FIFA knows very well that there is such a thing as the "law." And so it goes about creating ways to flout it. Everyone knows that for teams to be owned by multiple parties can't be a good thing, because of the conflicts of interest it generates. FIFA condemns the practice, but only acts if the majority of clubs within any federation demands it; that is, the law is only applied at the request of the clients.

And in the real world? In most cases, anyone who owns several teams also owns the odd TV channel. Is it really likely that a majority of club owners are going to try and cause rifts with the company selling the rights to broadcast their matches? Hardly. Which means that in practice someone can be the owner of various clubs though they are also the owner of the company that broadcasts the matches.

In 2015, for the first time in history, the US did something exemplary in the world of football. Not a move on the pitch but one in the world of finance: the FBI looked into alleged money laundering by FIFA representatives. Seven top CONCACAF officials were charged with having been receiving kickbacks over a period of twenty-five years. This provided legal evidence of something journalists had long been talking about.

For the conspiracy theorists, the investigation that toppled Blatter and his flunkies isn't actually about the letter of the law, but rather a move by the US to take control of an increasingly lucrative venture. If the network that controlled CONCACAF is dismantled, certain "windows of opportunity" are bound to present themselves in the region.

Clearly, while the players work up a sweat on the pitch, there are those involved in trafficking up in the members' boxes. Blatter's response to the FBI was to reveal his authoritarian streak. He didn't trouble himself with resigning. His view of the scandal was that it was a "regional issue" and one that could be brought to heel. And yet the bribes in question, when analyzed, showed clear leanings: when the voting behavior of the accused was looked at, they were all in Blatter's favor.

With no Figo to oppose him, the Swiss autocrat stood in the elections and won. Michel Platini, the head of UEFA, enjoined him to step down, but to no avail. The only thing that prompted Blatter to call a new election (though he put it off until February 2016) was new charges being brought against the men who had been arrested and the announcement of new lines of investigation.

How different from the goodbye of one great footballer. In the summer of 2015, upon retiring, Xavi Hernández, possibly the greatest Spanish player of all time, defined his job as "a ball and some guys running around after it." The words of a great. On behalf of this dream, FIFA does its business deals.

In art and sport alike we make a mental return to childhood, the space in which great marvels are possible. The unfortunate thing is that FIFA has put childhood up for sale.

THE FUTURE OF THE GAME: "ADVANCE TO THE BACK"

In an attempt to explain certain social phenomena, the philosopher Leszek Kołakowski quoted the tram conductor in old Warsaw who used to shout at the passengers, "Advance to the back!" The objective isn't always up ahead.

Football is modernity sick. What started out as a game now belongs to the industry of the spectacle, and FIFA runs theme parks that it happens to call football stadiums.

Football's true thrust is a backward trajectory, a nudge in the direction of the child we once were or, collectively, toward the origin of community life—the first tribes to use their feet in certain decisive ways, the horde dazzled by the flickering flames, compact and superstitious, disposed to support those who had a certain kind of stripe marked on their bodies and not others.

Two of the most well-known proponents of this idea (Eduardo Galeano in his *Football in Sun and Shadow* and Manuel Vázquez Montalbán in *A Religion in Search of a God*) emphasize the essential simplicity of a game governed by few rules, one that can be played barefoot and that requires of its players more nous than athletic predisposition.

The best thing about this joy-turned-money-spinner is returning mentally to the age when there could still be heroes and you did things for the sake of it. In a moral sense, the future of the game is in its past.

Is there any way for football, in its institutionalized form, to go back to its starting point? The 2015 Champions League Final presented a curious contrast between the brandy-quaffing prawn-sandwich eaters and the ultimate protagonists of the game.

FIFA had just been unmasked. Until that moment, the VIP balcony had been the least vulnerable zone in the sport; it was on the pitch that the unexpected would happen.

We fans love to be surprised; we know no one can really predict the way a game will go, except for maybe an old lady with no interest in the game but blessed by Lady Luck, or Paul, the German octopus who guessed the results of the 2006 World Cup.

When Juventus and Barcelona met in the final, football had gone topsy-turvy. All the surprises were no longer taking place on the pitch, but in the offices where the executives were being investigated. And that was perhaps why the players wanted to show that, in moments of crises of values, the best thing you can do is place your faith in tradition. Guided by a mysterious compensatory law, the protagonists of the game's elite competition avoided all uncertainty. While only chaos theory could explain FIFA accountancy, the finalists followed a classical template. For ninety minutes they took part in an altogether orderly adventure. The logic that reigned over the scoreboard was in direct contrast to the inexplicable sums of the men at the top.

Neither side was in the Berlin final by mistake. Both Juve and Barca had won league and cup doubles in their domestic competitions. The winner here would be no upstart. And even so, Barcelona were the clear favorites, and everything went as predicted, with the Catalans running out 3–1 winners.

A symbolic inversion had taken hold of the game: startling developments at the desks, none in the penalty area. Barca and Juve confirmed that tradition was still alive and well—by doing exactly what was expected.

It could be that we were witnessing a signal, one to say that the game's future lies in its origins; that is, in the people taking part. There's no going back to the times when a poor working-class mother washed the team strips and when players weren't paid for their time, but it has become extremely pressing now that the decision making be put in the hands of those who have themselves stood alongside the howling fans, who know the sufferings inside a dressing room, and who have actually sweated for a team. Michel Platini is one possible successor to Blatter, and Luis Figo also has the chance to become a central figure again.

An industry that depends on TV consortia, the holy war between Nike and Adidas, and the vast swathe of sponsors and government agencies who have a hand in running World Cups can never be entirely honest, but it can still bear a closer resemblance to what happens on the pitch. It is incumbent on the people who run the game that they emulate the players, in the same way that the players are emulating their childhood selves.

That cry of Kołakowski's conductor is worth remembering because it contains a sociological key. Football's destiny is also on that tram: "Advance to the back!"

ABOUT THE AUTHOR AND TRANSLATOR

JUAN VILLORO's journalistic and literary work has been recognized with such international prizes as the Premio Herralde de Novela, Premio Xavier Villaurrutia, el Premio Rey de España, el Premio Ciudad de Barcelona, and el Vázquez Montalbán de Periodismo Deportivo y el Antonin Artaud. He has been a professor of literature at la Universidad Nacional Autónoma de México, Yale, and la Universidad Pompeu Fabra de Barcelona. He is a columnist for the newspapers *Reforma* and *El Periódico de Catalunya*.

THOMAS BUNSTEAD's translations from the Spanish include work by Eduardo Halfon and Yuri Herrera, Aixa de la Cruz's story "True Milk" in *Best of European Fiction 2015*, and *A Brief History of Portable Literature* by Enrique Vila-Matas (a co-translation with Anne McLean). A guest editor of a Words Without Borders feature on Mexico (March 2015), Thomas has also published his own writing in the *Times Literary Supplement*, *The Independent*, the *Paris Review* blog, 3ammagazine.com, Days of Roses, ReadySteadyBook, and >kill author.

RESTLESS BOOKS is an independent publisher for readers and writers in search of new destinations, experiences, and perspectives. From Asia to the Americas, from Tehran to Tel Aviv, we deliver stories of discovery, adventure, dislocation, and transformation.

Our readers are passionate about other cultures and other languages. Restless is committed to bringing out the best of international literature—fiction, journalism, memoirs, poetry, travel writing, illustrated books, and more—that reflects the restlessness of our multiform lives.

Visit us at www.restlessbooks.com.